THE
COMPLETE
ARTHRITIS
HANDBOOK

Anne Charlish

Published in Great Britain MCMXCVI by Carnell Ltd,
28 Charles Square, London N1 6HT

Copyright © MCMXCVI by Carnell Ltd.

Typeset by SJ Design and Publishing, Bromley, Kent.

Printed by Repro City Limited, London.

ISBN 1-85779-125-8

Table of Contents

Introduction   5

Arthritis: What Really Works?   9

How Can You Tell It's Arthritis – And Which Type?   19

Relief From Pain: What Works?   24

Exercises That Work   47

Eat What Works   59

Special Treatments That Work   75

What Can The Doctors Do To Help You?   90

Devices And Gadgets   116

Conclusion   132

The introduction which follows has been provided by Dr F Dudley Hart.

F Dudley Hart, MD, FRCP, Consultant Physician and Rheumatologist, Westminster Hospital, Consultant Physician, Hospital of St John and St Elizabeth, London. Member of Executive and Finance Committee, Arthritis and Rheumatism Council; Honorary Fellow Royal Society of Medicine and British Society for Rheumatology. Editor of *French's Index of Differential Diagnosis, Clinical Rheumatology Illustrated, Drug Treatment of the Rheumatic Diseases, Practical Problems in Rheumatology* and for the patient, *Overcoming Arthritis*.

Introduction

I am very pleased to write an introduction to this book. No other group of disorders causes so much discomfort and disorganisation of one's life as the more chronic arthritic disorders and few go on for such a painfully long time. They may not in general be as dangerous to life as many other diseases, but they often go on for longer periods of time. It is extraordinary, therefore, that there have not been more books written in non-medical terms for the poor, suffering patients themselves to help them know more about the condition from which they suffer and about what they can do to help themselves. These disorders have always been so common that in the past they have often been regarded as natural to mankind and therefore tolerated without complaint. Rheumatology has only become an accepted Speciality in Medicine in most countries in the western world in the last sixty years or so, and there have only been academic units with Professors of Rheumatology in this country since the last world war.

What is rheumatism? In previous years, rheumatic fever was not an uncommon condition in childhood, with flitting pains going from joint to joint after a throat infection due to a particular streptococcus. Some of these unfortunate children developed heart disease, which could be (and often was) fatal. With improved living conditions and less overcrowding, this disease was becoming less common, but with the advent of sulphur drugs just before World War II and penicillin after the war, it became a rarity in this country. The term 'rheumatism' is, however, still widely used in a lay sense to refer to any aching, painful process anywhere in muscles, bones, joints and ligaments, but it has no specific medical meaning. Many of these symptoms can be due to fatigue, stress, unhappiness or some other similar condition rather than any specific disease process. But there are today, as the author mentions, some 200 or more conditions where aches and pains are due to actual disease of bones, joints, ligaments and muscles. These disorders may, particularly if long-lasting, become accompanied by crippling, anxiety and depression. Many of these 'rheumatic' arthritic disorders, in fact the vast majority, are of short duration, lead to no chronic changes in the joints and are followed by complete recovery. Many follow some infection and recovery occurs in a few days or weeks, as can happen, for instance, after German measles (rubella). Many are due to injuries or strains to muscles, joints or ligaments. The term 'arthritis', as the author says, means inflammation of tissues of the joint, the term arthrosis refers to primarily non-inflammatory joint disease. But even here, inflammatory changes can result from degenerative changes, as in the commonest joint disorder of all, osteoarthritis.

We all have over 200 joints, large and small, in arms, legs, spine and pelvis and any of these can be injured, strained, infected or inflamed. All are plentifully supplied with nerves which tell us that something is wrong by causing discomfort and pain. These painful sensations are carried to our brains and sometimes to other parts of our bodies or extremities and can cause diagnostic confusion and worry.

What are the most common types of arthritis? Some degenerative changes occur in all of us as we age. While these are usually painless, some aches and pains do occur in most of us at some time in our lives, though perhaps only 20 to 25 per cent of us ever have to see our general practitioners because of them. As the author says on the first page, some 20 million people in Great Britain will at some time in their lives have symptoms arising from joints, but only about 8 million will need to consult their doctors. Rheumatoid arthritis affects between 1 per cent and 2 per cent of the population, being two or three times more common in women than in men. The so-called sero-negative types of inflammatory arthritis, where blood tests for rheumatoid factor are negative, are not uncommon. These include the types of arthritis associated with chronic colitis, psoriasis and the variety where the spine is affected by inflammatory change, ankylosing spondylitis. Some types of arthritis follow infections of gut or urinary tract, the so-called post-infective arthropathies to distinguish them from the rarer infective arthropathies where the infecting organism can be isolated from the joint. There are a few potentially serious types of arthritis, but even these, like rheumatoid arthritis or systemic lupus erythematosus, can occur in mild form.

It is important, therefore, to get the correct diagnosis made early so that appropriate measures can be initiated early in the course of the disease. With so many different varieties, treatments differ with different disorders, and even within one diagnosis with different patients as the same condition can affect different patients in different ways.

Early diagnosis should be followed by an explanation to the patient of what the treatment involves and how he or she can assist in the therapeutic programme. This early education of the patient in his or her treatment is what this book is all about. Gone are the days when one was only told "You've got arthritis. It's chronic. There is no real treatment. You've got to learn to live with it". We have now so many more medicines, different forms of physical treatment and surgical measures available that even if you have a chronic arthritis much benefit can be obtained. A practical book like this will prove very helpful to many. Happily, a considerable number of arthritic disorders settle down and abate naturally, Father Time and Mother Nature together effecting a cure, but even then painful symptoms need the appropriate treatment for a time, while exercise and activities may need to be controlled. This book will, I am sure, prove very helpful, nay invaluable, to sufferers with many different forms of arthritis.

Dr F Dudley Hart
London, 1993

1 Arthritis: What Really Works?

WHAT IS MEANT BY 'ARTHRITIS'?

Popular names for aches and pains are subject to fashion. Fifty years ago everyone said they suffered from rheumatics or lumbago. Then it was the turn of neuralgia, or sciatica; still later everybody's backache became a slipped disc. These days the popular term is arthritis or rheumatism, unless you are a sportsman, and then you probably claim to suffer from 'cartilage trouble'. The fact is that it is perfectly natural to have a few aches and pains or stiffness from time to time, at any age and more especially as your body gets older. Physical change can take place without you necessarily becoming ill, disabled, or even noticeably aware of it. In fact, the terms arthritis and rheumatism are so general every one of us probably experiences one of the symptoms covered by them at some time in our lives.

Taking arthritis and rheumatism together (to begin with they are quite difficult to tell apart): some 20 million people in Britain will experience some form or other each year. About eight million consult their doctor about it and 25% of all those consulting their doctor will probably have either arthritis or rheumatism. These diseases account for one third of all severely disabled people in Britain. Some form of arthritis may affect as many as one person in five at some time of their life. It is the biggest single cause of disability in the country today and costs the NHS huge sums in drugs and therapy. It also accounts for the loss of 88 million working days. Add to this an untold account of human suffering and disability: all the aches, pains, stiffness, restricted mobility and enforced dependence of those who suffer from this all too common disease. Small wonder that the hunt for improved treatments and above all, some cure for arthritis, is a prime concern of medical and drug research.

Like many conditions that are widespread, incurable, but inclined to come and go inexplicably, myths and old wives' tales cling to the subject of arthritis; about what causes it and what makes it worse or better. It is the purpose of this book to try and sort scientific fact from fiction and to give those who suffer from it, especially those with the more crippling forms of the disease, some insight into what it is and how best to manage it. Understanding gives some degree of control; knowing what may and what certainly won't happen, makes it easier to face the future and to take a constructive approach to a group of illnesses that don't kill, but which can make life desperately uncomfortable.

WHAT IS ARTHRITIS?

Arthritis is trouble with your joints. The word itself is a combination of 'art(h)', meaning something joined or put together and 'itis', meaning inflammation. That said, a troublesome joint is not always inflamed and so you will hear doctors use the more precise term arthrosis as well, meaning a condition of the joints.

Of course when you feel pain or stiffness, unless you are medically trained, you don't necessarily know what's causing it: it could be a joint, strained muscle, ligament, trapped nerve or even a bruise. You probably try to think what you may have done to cause the problem, and this search for explanation – which is a quite natural desire to control what happens to you, to put it right or avoid it happening again – will colour what you decide to call your problem. That is how terms like arthritis and rheumatism come to be applied to a vast range of physical aches or discomfort that may be nothing to do with joints at all.

A human joint is a complicated and delicately balanced piece of engineering composed of several components acting together. You don't need to understand it as well as a doctor does, but since the different forms of arthritis produce different symptoms and call for different treatment, it will help you to know a little about how joints work when fit and what goes wrong when they are poorly.

A joint is a place where bones meet and move against each other. The word 'articulated', which we use more frequently about lorries or speech, can be used to describe the human skeleton, making use of the same 'art' prefix, meaning 'joined', that we find in arthritis. The skeleton is a jointed framework that supports the body and enables it to perform a fantastic range of movements, swift and powerful, fine and delicate, twisting, leaping, bending and lifting. These movements are controlled by *muscles, tendons* and *ligaments* attached to the bones, which can thereby be rearranged in relation to one another to accomplish a wide range of actions and positions – stretching above your head to reach a high shelf; crouching down to hide under the table. Where the ends of bones move against each other they are cushioned by a layer of *cartilage* (rather as soft metal bearings cushion the movement of hard metal parts), and *fluid*, like the lubricant used to bathe the moving parts of an engine.

In most cases the whole joint is encased in a capsule or sheath which is rich with *nerve endings* which communicate with the brain – the reason why it is so painful when joints are damaged or inflamed. Outside this sometimes are *ligaments* to stabilise the joint: hold it firmly in position and limit its range. There is one more part worth being familiar with: the little pads between the muscle and the joint capsule called *bursae* – the Latin for little bags or purses. These act rather like shock absorbers to cushion the joint from the stress of sudden or strong movement – jumping, kicking, lifting great weights. The bursae become swollen and inflamed under excessive use or pressure and give the general name *bursitis* to a group of occupationally-related forms of arthritis like Housemaid's or Priest's Knee (a lot of time spent kneeling) or Student's Elbow (from writing too long at a hard desk). There used to be a condition known in Britain as Weaver's Bottom which resulted from spending too long sitting on a hard seat in front of a weaving loom. Not surprisingly, that is now even rarer than Housemaid's Knee.

In an unhealthy or ageing joint this smooth interaction breaks down. In *osteoarthritis* the cartilage becomes thin and flaky and begins to split. The bone underneath becomes thicker and eventually starts to project at the edges of the joint almost as if it were trying to reduce the amount of movement possible. The amount of fluid in the joint increases, leading to swelling, stiffness and pain; the capsule encasing the joint is stretched. In severe osteoarthritis the cartilage may wear away completely exposing the bone underneath; or chalky deposits of crystals may form in it which can break off and float around in the fluid. The joint may become permanently deformed.

In *rheumatoid arthritis* inflammation starts in the membrane surrounding the joint (the synovium), which then thickens and begins to occupy the space within the joint. The inflammation spreads to the rest of the joint capsule, and the ligaments and tendons that surround and support it become stretched so that the joint may become unstable. If the inflammation remains unchecked the cartilage in the joint will shrink and the exposed ends of the bone become eaten away leading to still further deformation.

This is a simple outline of how arthritis affects joints. Joints differ considerably; some, like the hip are more flexible, with all-round rotation, than say the elbow, which only goes backward and forward. In the spine the interconnected vertebrae have even less independent movement and are jointed without a capsule or lubricating fluid. This leaves the disc of cushioning cartilage between them with an even more crucial role to play and contributes to back-pain being the most widespread and intractable form of joint pain human beings can suffer.

WHAT KIND OF ARTHRITIS?

There are more than 200 forms of arthritis though many of these are rare. Some are mild, some severe; some get worse, some come and go, some disappear altogether. It is possible to break arthritis down into families under headings of the processes involved:

Wear and tear or degenerative arthritis. This includes the most common form of arthritis – *osteoarthritis* ('osteo' is Latin for bone), or 'degenerative joint disease' which has the advantage of being plain English, but the disadvantage of suggesting that only the elderly suffer from it. Joints, like the moving parts of a motor car or washing machine, wear out and perform less reliably with heavy use or just with the passage of time. When they start to give trouble will depend on the quality of the basic components and the stresses and strains to which they are subjected. Translated into human terms, this means you may get osteoarthritis because your cartilage is the kind that becomes thin and flaky with age, or because you have crucified your joints on the sportsfield, or imposed excessive strain upon them by loading them with too much body weight, or even because you had the not uncommon misfortune to be born with two legs not of exactly the same length.

That is not to say that osteoarthritis is an inevitable consequence of ageing. Some people's bones and joints are old at forty; some youthful at seventy. None of us ages at the same rate. Nevertheless, live long enough and 90% of us develop some degree of osteoarthritis – though it may give you little trouble because with increasing age we make fewer demands on our bodies.

Inflammation. The most common of this kind of arthritis is *rheumatoid arthritis*. In this illness the cause of joint inflammation is unknown. It may be sparked off by infection with a virus – such as scarlet fever – but often it is as though the body's defence mechanisms have turned against themselves and perpetuate the inflammation even in the absence of any harmful germ. The dauntingly named *ankylosing spondylitis* of the spine (ankylosis means 'stiffening' and spondyl is a Greek word for the joints in the spine plus 'itis' for inflammation: an inflammatory condition of the spine that leads to stiffening) is another form of inflammatory arthritis. It is one of a group that includes *reactive arthritis* – which usually follows an infection (this includes Reiter's disease, where the eyes also become inflamed), *psoriatic arthritis* (associated with the skin condition psoriasis) and *colitic arthritis* (affecting the colon: the end of the digestive tract) – all of which are fortunately quite rare.

A breakdown in body chemistry. The most common of these diseases is *gout,* in which the joint becomes inflamed because the body fails to break down harmful crystals of uric acid which form inside the joint causing intense pain. *Pseudo (false) gout* is a similar, less severe condition in which calcium phosphate crystals develop in the cartilage lining the joints.

Other kinds of arthritic disease are a mixture of both inflammation and wear and tear. In addition it can be caused by bacterial infection (septic arthritis) or may be associated with a more general physical infection. Some forms of arthritis more than others run in families and may be traced to a particular gene – HLA B27. However, there is no form that is entirely hereditary.

No form of arthritis is infectious and having one kind does not predispose you to catching another.

WHO GETS IT, WHERE AND WHY?

Not surprisingly with such a chameleon of a disease, different forms of arthritis affect different groups of people. Some are more common in men or in women, in certain age-groups or among people with particular jobs or hobbies. They also affect different joints. In the vast majority of cases, the exact cause of the disease is still a mystery, though a number of factors that make arthritis more likely are known.

Osteoarthritis. About five million people in this country are affected and although many suffer little pain or restricted activity, it always shows up on an X-ray. The condition has been common to mankind since prehistory and affects other animals with a similar sort of skeleton.

Osteoarthritis related to ageing cartilage usually starts in the 50s, but it can begin as early as the 30s. It is most common among middle-aged women and the elderly. However, it is also a major problem for young sportsmen, football and rugby players in particular, as a result of exceptional joint injuries during play.

The joints most commonly affected are the spine – especially the vertebrae at the base of the neck and below the waist (the lumbar region); the knees (rather more common in women than men); the hip (affects both sexes equally but often shows up earlier than knee arthritis); the hands (more common in women, often around the time of the menopause); the foot, particularly the joint at the base of the big toe (the one most distorted by the wearing of enclosed shoes), also more common in women. With the exception of the hands these are all parts of the skeleton that take the strain of carrying us about and holding us upright: load-bearing joints. These joints seem to be particularly vulnerable to osteoarthritis. They are also vulnerable to injury and some form of injury in childhood or youth can often be traced to a joint developing osteoarthritis in later life. This is not to say that injury always causes osteoarthritis. Most injured joints repair themselves satisfactorily with no sign of subsequent deterioration.

Although there is no suggestion that this form of arthritis is inherited, a tendency to age rapidly or to wear well certainly runs in families (the age our parents die as well as what they die of is an indicator of when we will probably die and what of). This may be connected with how well our bones, muscle, cartilage and other connective tissue repair and take wear in their stride.

Rheumatoid arthritis. One million people in this country suffer from rheumatoid arthritis: between 1% and 2% of the population. It is the commonest inflammatory disease affecting the joints and is a much more distressing illness than osteoarthritis both in the short and long term. It can strike at any age, including in childhood, but starts most frequently in youth or early middle age. It affects all races and all climes but tends to be more severe in Northern Europe and affects three times as many women as men.

People who contract rheumatoid arthritis may have a single acute attack that persists for several months, or longer but which then clears up and never reappears again; or it may continue to plague them for the rest of their life, when it is chronic. Fortunately only in a few cases does the disease persist to the point of becoming severely crippling.

The joints most commonly affected are the hands, arms and legs. It usually, but not invariably, affects both sides symmetrically. Occasionally it affects the jaw, but only rarely the spine.

The causes of rheumatoid arthritis are also uncertain. Studies of identical twins who contract the same illnesses when these are linked to the genes they are born with, suggest that there is a genetic component in the disease – perhaps 30% – but there is no obvious environmental factor to explain the remaining 70% of cases. An increasing number of medical experts think that the illness may turn out to have been sparked off by infection from some unknown or unnoted virus. There is some evidence that it is less severe these days in the UK and the USA which might be explained by people being less frequently exposed to infectious diseases in childhood, thanks to improved vaccination programmes.

Gout. For some reason – perhaps because it is associated with portly middle-aged gentlemen who have lived not wisely but too well – this extremely painful form of arthritis is traditionally a popular subject for cartoons. "More rich than poor, more wise than fools . . ." were susceptible, observed an 18th century doctor. In fact, gout is no laughing matter and does not confine its attentions to bon viveurs, although it does afflict those of more than average intelligence and may be aggravated by certain foods and alcoholic drinks like port and red wine. It is more common among men at all ages, but can affect women after the menopause. Today it is one of the better understood forms of arthritis and the one most easily treated.

The most commonly affected joint is well known: the big toe. But other joints – the knee, elbow or the wrists – may be attacked too. The culprit is uric acid crystals forming inside the joint. Uric acid is a normal waste product found dissolved in the blood of healthy people and disposed of through their kidneys. Even if the level is high – and men usually have higher levels than women – it will not necessarily lead to gout. A tendency to high levels of uric acid is inherited, but not everyone with high levels in a family develops gout. As in many diseases for which you may inherit susceptibility, like heart disease, something in your environment is still required to trigger an attack. It is only when the uric acid turns into crystals inside the joint that problems arise. If you are subject to gout, an injury as slight as a bruise, worry, fatigue, illness or becoming run-down, even a minor operation like having a tooth out, may set off an attack. Excessive eating and drinking, especially of special danger list foods, can also trigger an attack. Conversely, an obese person who suffers gout may experience an attack following a crash diet. Diuretics can trigger an attack in women after the time of the menopause.

Pseudo gout. The joint most commonly affected is the knee. The formation of calcium crystals in the cartilage lining the joint is thought to be quite common as people grow older. It is quite harmless unless the crystals become dislodged, in which case they can also set up inflammation in the joint, less painful than in gout, which is usually treated by anti-inflammatory drugs or by drawing off the fluid containing the crystals with a syringe. Only if the swelling and inflammation are neglected can the disease cause long-term damage.

Ankylosing spondylitis. This is a relatively uncommon form of arthritis (affecting about 1 person in 1,000), mainly young men. A few women develop it, though usually mildly, and sometimes school-age children show the early signs of the disease, but the most likely time of onset is between 17 and 27. It is inflammatory, though quite distinct from rheumatoid arthritis, and affects principally the spine, although the hips, knees and ankles can also be involved. To begin with you experience stiffness caused by the inflammation but as this dies down and healing takes place, bone grows out from either side of the affected vertebrae and may eventually grow together (the fusing implied by the word ankylosis) leading to a rigid 'poker' spine. This was more common in the past than today when better medical understanding has led to more appropriate treatment.

The exact cause of ankylosing spondylitis is not known, but we do know that it runs in families and that 90% of those who get it carry a particular gene called HLA B27. But only one person in twenty who carries this gene actually contracts the disease, so the most likely explanation is that something in the environment, at present unknown, triggers an attack in those at risk. It may follow unusual exertion or strain which at first will be blamed, but ankylosing spondylitis is definitely not caused by athletic activity. It is one of a group of inflammatory forms of arthritis known collectively as 'seronegative' arthritis, because the distinctive rheumatoid antibody – the marker of rheumatoid arthritis (*see symptoms in Chapter 2*), is not found in the blood serum of patients with these diseases. Other rare seronegative forms are reactive arthritis, Reiter's disease, psoriatic and colitic arthritis in which arthritis occasionally occurs following an infection. The infections themselves may be mild or almost without symptoms, so that special medical tests are needed to show up the cause of the arthritis.

Psoriasis is a relatively uncommon (1% - 2% of the population) skin disease of varying severity. Arthritis afflicts one in ten of sufferers and is usually limited to just a few joints: the spine, neck, or the end joints of the fingers and toes. Fortunately it is rarely crippling. Although it tends to run in families, it appears to be triggered by something in the environment.

2 How Can You Tell It's Arthritis -- And Which Type?

Chapter 1 has outlined how the various kinds of arthritis affect the joints; this chapter focuses on the symptoms experienced if you get these diseases: the patient's eye view. We will concentrate on the early signs; further down the line you probably know what you have because your doctor puts a name to it. We will outline the way symptoms can develop as arthritis progresses. Forewarned is forearmed and knowing what to expect will enable you to cope with your condition constructively and positively.

WHAT IS NOT ARTHRITIS?

We don't want to encourage anyone to be a hypochondriac, but neither do we want you to suffer in silence when relief and understanding are just around the corner. Arthritis is not:

- sporting injury, a pulled muscle, torn ligament, whip-lash or other accidental (traumatic) damage to your joints or body which cause temporary pain;
- muscular pain or stiffness following unaccustomed physical activity such as heavy gardening, moving furniture;
- Tennis, Golfer's, Cresta (tobogganing) or any other of the painful, occupationally-named 'Elbows' which result from the inflammation of the projecting bone at the side of the elbow caused by excessive use;
- Housemaid's Knee (better called 'Spring-cleaning Knee' these days), or Student's Elbow, following prolonged pressure on a hard surface;

- aches and pains associated with influenza or other common viral infections;
- pain or stiffness following sleep in an uncomfortable position or sitting in a cold draught.

You will see that what these harmless, but uncomfortable aches and pains have in common is that they can be traced to a definite, exceptional event or activity and they get better given time and rest.

Arthritis causes persistent pain, stiffness and difficulty in using the affected joint, not related to a particular, recent event. Sometimes there is swelling, tenderness or heat in the joint and you may also feel tired, sluggish or generally unwell. Some types of arthritis give you a fever, a rash or other symptoms. Needless to say, if you suffer from joint pain and these latter symptoms you should see your doctor straight away. It is probably also true to say that if your pain has been bad enough for you to take standard painkillers like paracetamol two or more times a week for a month, you should also consult her. But some people don't like taking painkillers and some notice pain less than others, so this is not an infallible guide. Delaying treatment, if you do have arthritis, can lead to complications or things getting worse, and the treatment (*described in Chapter 7*) will then be different. To help you decide, we will list the early (and later) symptoms of arthritis for each type.

Osteoarthritis. The commonest kind of joint disorder will probably affect us all if we live long enough, though it will not necessarily need medical treatment more complicated than taking painkillers in response to pain, controlling your weight and keeping up regular exercise.

If osteoarthritis starts when you are still young (under 40) and is related to a joint which you know you injured some time ago, you are more likely to notice it than if it creeps up on you in middle age and is more generalised. To begin with the pain, stiffness and restriction of movement that it causes will only bother you occasionally and will get better with rest. The joint may become noisy, creaking or crunching and even alarming your friends – this is called crepitation. This is because the cartilage – the gristly lining that cushions bone inside a joint – roughens with wear and tear and no longer moves as silently and smoothly as before. Your symptoms will come and go; damp weather could aggravate things, as will exercise, so they will probably be worse at the end of the day, but you could also notice stiffness first thing in the morning or after resting the joint for any time. There is often slight swelling which can be either bony (in a big toe joint subject to recurrent bunions) or fluid (knees and ankles). In some cases the pain even bothers you at rest or during the night. The infuriating thing is no one is absolutely certain what causes this pain and stiffness. The good news is that it is almost always treatable.

If you describe your symptoms to a doctor, she will instantly recognise the creaking, the swelling and the restriction of movement that is typical of osteoarthritis. The thinning of cartilage and the beginning of bone changes will also show up on an X-ray, though there is no blood test for the disease. At the early stages there is little that tells you or your doctor how severe it may become. Some joints, especially the hip or knee, become so painful and disabling that surgical replacement may be recommended. In other cases the disease peaks a few years after symptoms become noticeable and either stays the same or becomes a little easier. This is a good reason to remain positive and optimistic if you are given a diagnosis of osteoarthritis.

Rheumatoid arthritis. The onset is usually gradual. The first symptoms are commonly felt in the fingers, wrists or balls of the feet. The affected joints become uncomfortable, may swell and become stiff, particularly first thing in the morning. Most people feel tired, off colour and rather irritable or depressed. Occasionally the first attack is severe with several joints affected accompanied by a slight fever, and weight loss, and you may feel patently unwell.

The good news is that 30% of people with rheumatoid arthritis recover completely within months, or at most years, and never suffer again. The more likely pattern is that you will have flare-ups off and on for the rest of your life. Fortunately, however, only 5% to 10% of those affected develop severely disabling disease.

You should certainly see your doctor with an attack of rheumatoid arthritis. In addition to the characteristic pattern of swelling and stiffness, she may discover other symptoms of the disease, outside the affected joints: nodules sometimes develop, and the inflammation can affect the lungs and eyes. The doctor will take a blood sample which enables her to chart the progress of the inflammation, and may also reveal the presence of a special antibody called 'rheumatoid factor', characteristic of the disease (though not absolutely everyone with rheumatoid arthritis produces it) or the side-effect of anaemia – a reduction in the number of important oxygen-carrying red corpuscles.

Gout. An acute attack of gout usually starts at night with pain in the big toe, though the knee, wrist and elbow may also be involved. The toe will be red, swollen and extremely tender; even rubbing it against the bed clothes may wake you with the pain. Occasionally a bad bunion can be mistaken for gout, but a blood test at the doctor's surgery will reveal higher than normal levels of uric acid and suggest the diagnosis of gout. To be certain, the doctor will withdraw some of the fluid surrounding the affected joint with a needle. Under the microscope uric acid crystals in the fluid will show up confirming the diagnosis. Once you know that you have a tendency to gout you must be on the lookout for early signs of an attack which can be triggered by minor injury and stress as well as over-indulgence in forbidden uric-acid-rich food and drink.

Ankylosing spondylitis. This can easily be mistaken for common-or-garden backache to start with. Pain from the inflamed vertebrae of the spine may be referred to your bottom or the back of your thighs. In other words, although the cause is in one place (the spine), you actually feel the pain somewhere else. Exceptionally for arthritis, ankylosing spondylitis often follows some form of physical exertion or strain, though it isn't caused by it. The stiff back, worse in the early morning, which is characteristic of the condition is only rarely inca-pacitating and you may carry on with mild aches and pains for some time. Occasionally other limb joints are involved or you may become tender under the heel or bottom, making sitting or standing on hard surfaces uncomfortable. There are still rarer complications affecting the heart, lungs, nervous system or the eye.

Typically, a doctor sees someone with ankylosing spondylitis when they have been suffering for some years. A blood test and X-rays of the spine may indicate the presence of inflammatory disease and distinguish it from ordinary backache. Once the doctor suspects ankylosing spondylitis she can order a special antibody test which will reveal the presence of the HLA B27 antigen, a gene carried by 90% of sufferers. Ankylosing spondylitis usually starts when you are young, and although it often comes and goes over long periods, nearly always settles down in the long run, although the stiffening persists.

Juvenile arthritis. Some 15,000 children develop arthritis in Britain every year. One form is very like adult rheumatoid arthritis, but another, which is accompanied by a rash and fever, can easily be confused with measles. A child with arthritis is clearly very ill and you will want to consult your doctor immediately. She will make a diagnosis and take responsibility for the child's treatment. Although juvenile rheumatoid arthritis is distressing and wearying, it is a less unpleasant disorder than the adult type. In any twelve children with the disease, only one will develop the adult type and only one later develops ankylosing spondylitis.

OTHER SYMPTOMS OF ARTHRITIS

There are more than 200 forms of arthritis, most of them quite rare. Some are accompanied by skin rashes or inflammation of the mouth, eyes or areas of mucous membrane (the smooth lining found inside the mouth and other body cavities). What the affected areas have in common is that they are all kinds of connective tissue, and, although to us they seem very different, they are often affected by similar disease processes. This is what gives arthritis such a chameleon complexion and makes the disease such a challenge for medical research.

3 Relief From Pain: What Works?

Living with arthritis is not easy. It means adapting your life to the limitations put on you by your disease and, above all, it means learning to minimise and cope with the pain.

Pain is very wearing. It has a greater effect on you than you could ever know before it became your constant companion. But there are many things you can do that will help you deal with it.

In the past, all too often patients were told, "There's no cure", and, "You'll have to learn to live with it". There is not much comfort in these words, particularly when patients are not even told just how they might learn to live with it.

That's what this chapter aims to do. Patients need to take responsibility for their own bodies, their own diseases, their treatment and their future.

None of the things suggested here will work for everyone. But many of them are known to work for some people.

And that might include you. So start here and think positive.

REST

If you feel you are in need of a rest, take one. Everyone needs to rest at times and, if you suffer from arthritis, you are likely to need more than most. So never be afraid or ashamed to take the rest you need.

Too much heavy work, or too strenuous activity, may actually cause damage to affected joints. That is not to say, however, that you should avoid exercise (*see Chapter 4*). There will probably be times when you feel you need to rest a joint, and times when you find that you have been sitting or lying down for too long and that you feel stiff.

The secret is to find the balance between rest and exercise that suits you. No two people need exactly the same amounts of either, so it is up to you to discover what is best for you.

BED REST

If you are suffering from severe pain, the only answer may be complete bed rest for a while. This is never an appealing prospect, particularly for people who like to be active in both body and mind, and people often struggle on painfully for weeks or even months before they accept its necessity. In severe cases, sufferers may even be admitted to hospital for this reason alone. Bed rest may simply be the unavoidable price that needs to be paid for the relief of pain.

Complete bed rest means lying flat all day and getting up only for meals, going to the toilet and washing. Do not put pillows under your knees. If possible, place a board at the foot of the bed so as to keep the ankles at right angles to the body. The pressure of bedclothes on painful feet can be agonising so a cradle over the feet, under the bedclothes, can be beneficial. If you do not have such a thing at home, a makeshift version can be made using a large cardboard box, with two adjacent sides removed.

Bed rest may be necessary for a few days, even, in rare cases, for several weeks in really severe rheumatoid arthritis, before pain is relieved. Some problems, however, may actually improve within just a few days, after which it will be possible to return gradually to a normal way of life. Even then, a series of rests throughout the day can be helpful. Never be afraid to take a rest; a lie down after lunch can make all the difference as to whether you feel you can cope with the rest of the day ahead.

STRESS

Some people tend to develop arthritis after periods of prolonged worry and then to suffer 'flareups' at particularly stressful times. Pain and suffering can also seem a lot worse if you also feel under pressure. It is therefore most important to manage the stress in your life.

Some stress is an unavoidable part of living and the answer lies not in eliminating it altogether from your life but rather in learning to cope with it. That means learning to relax.

RELAXATION

Relaxation is a skill and, like all other skills, it has to be learned and practised. No one method will suit everyone. Some people claim that they get all the relaxation they need from reading a good book or listening to music, but most people are actually a lot more tense than they realise and relaxing means rather more than just sitting down and taking it easy for a while.

Popular methods of relaxation include deep breathing, progressive relaxation, visualisation and meditation.

DEEP BREATHING

Breathing is an automatic function and we therefore don't think about it much. But, before you begin these exercises, it is worth recognising that there are, in fact, two quite distinct ways of breathing.

These are costal (meaning 'of the ribs') and abdominal. Costal breathing, which is seen by an outward, upward movement of the chest, is not the correct way to breathe, although it may come in useful during strenuous exercise.

Abdominal breathing, on the other hand, is the correct way to breathe. It is also an important tool in stress management. When you breathe in, the diaphragm, which is a strong, dome-shaped sheet of muscle between the chest cavity and the abdomen, contracts and pushes downwards, causing the abdomen to relax as the lungs expand. When you breathe out, the diaphragm relaxes, and the abdomen contracts as air is expelled from the lungs.

1. Lie on your back with your feet a comfortable distance apart. Close your eyes.
2. Put one hand on your abdomen so you can feel the movement of the abdominal muscles, and put the other one on your chest in order to check that there is little or no movement here.
3. Breathe slowly and deeply, inhaling and exhaling through the nostrils. You can exaggerate the normal breathing process by deliberately pulling in the abdominal muscles as you breathe out; you can even push your abdominal muscles in gently with your hand. As you breathe in, you should be aware of the abdominal muscles pushing out.
4. Practise this method of deep breathing for about five minutes each day until it becomes second nature to you. It should then become the natural way you breathe, in every position.

PROGRESSIVE RELAXATION

This is an excellent method of relaxation, which gradually works on both mind and body, working from the toes to the head.

1. Lie on your back with your feet a comfortable distance apart. Let your muscles relax so that your arms fall naturally away from your body and your legs fall comfortably away from each other.
2. Concentrate on your toes. Tense and clench them for about three seconds, then relax them. Slowly work your way up your legs, tensing and relaxing the calf muscles, then the knees, and finally the thighs. Now stretch out the full length of the legs and feet before relaxing them completely.

3. Turn your attention to the middle part of the body, clenching and releasing the buttocks, stomach muscles and hips in turn.
4. Work through the arms and hands in much the same way as you did with the feet and legs.
5. Hunch your shoulders and tighten the neck. Hold for about three seconds, then feel the tension flow away as you relax.
6. Then concentrate on your face, clenching and releasing in turn the jaw, eyes, eyebrows and forehead. Finally, breathe in and out deeply. You should now feel a heavy relaxed feeling in your entire body. Concentrate on your breathing, and on the cool air going in your nostrils and the warm air coming out of them. Maintain this relaxed state for several minutes.
7. Come out of relaxation slowly. Take a deep breath, feel the energy return to your arms and move your fingers slightly. Take another deep breath, feel the energy return to your legs and move your toes slightly. Stretch your arms and legs and slowly open your eyes. Roll to one side and sit up.

VISUALISATION

When you feel easy with progressive relaxation, perhaps after a couple of weeks, you can progress to the next stage and incorporate visualisation, which has the effect of relaxing not only the body but also the mind. This can be of great benefit in arthritis, a painful condition that can cause a lot of tension and therefore severe stress.

1. Practise progressive relaxation as above.
2. When you are completely relaxed, concentrate on letting your mind become quiet and still. Do not concentrate on any particular thought but rather on emptying your mind.
3. Imagine a peaceful scene, perhaps a deserted, warm beach, with an atmosphere of total calm and tranquillity.

4. Concentrate on the feelings of light, warmth, calm and peace and on the sensation of total relaxation they bring you.
5. Remain in this relaxed state for about five minutes. Then come out of it as described above for progressive relaxation.

MEDITATION

The aim of meditation, which has been practised in India and Asia for centuries, is to discipline the mind on one single thing to the exclusion of all others. This, it is believed, will lead to complete relaxation, which can in turn be of tremendous help in the relief of the tension and pain that are so often caused by arthritis.

It involves sitting in a quiet room and concentrating on just one thing. This may be an object, a fruit or flower, say; a word, which is known as a 'mantra'; or a bodily- generated rhythm such as breathing. It may sound simple but it is actually much more difficult than you may imagine.

If you want to learn to meditate, it is probably therefore best to join a special group where you can be taught to do it properly. You will then be able to do it at home and to incorporate it into your daily life.

EXERCISE

The question of rest or exercise remains a controversial one. For while rest can be as important as taking your medicine, so some exercise, in moderation, is absolutely essential.

Exercise is necessary for two main reasons:

• to keep muscles strong;
• to maintain a full range of movement.

No two sufferers are exactly the same and the important thing is therefore to find your own optimum balance between rest and exercise. It may take a little time to get that balance right.

Most patients continue to lead normal, active lives, and are able to do all the normal things they want to do. Many of them agree, however, that periods of rest are important, especially during a flare-up.

Basically, all joints should be put through their full range of movements, and that means as far as they can go in each direction every day, other than any acutely inflamed areas that are simply too painful to move. In general, little and often is better than any form of prolonged or strenuous exercise. At the first sign of increased pain, stop and try again the next day, but remember that it is better to do a little too much than to do nothing at all.

Don't allow yourself to be talked into anything too strenuous on the 'exercise is good for you' principle. It is, but not if it's going to make you feel worse. If in doubt, talk to your doctor or physiotherapist.

Specific remedial exercises are given in detail in Chapter 4.

SWIMMING

Swimming is a particularly good form of exercise for anyone, at any age, who suffers from arthritis. Swimming pools are nearly always heated and exercises in warm water encourage the muscles to relax as well as allowing joints to be put through a range of movements without putting any weight on them.

YOGA

Yoga is another good form of exercise for anyone who suffers from arthritis. An ancient Indian philosophy, it both strengthens the body and increases flexibility, as well as calming the mind and encouraging feelings of utmost relaxation.

It is difficult, some would say impossible, to learn yoga by yourself or even with the aid of a book. It is better to go to a class where you will be taught by a qualified teacher. You may then find you benefit from classes to such an extent that you want to continue going to them or, having learned the rudiments, you may feel able to practise on your own at home.

CHOOSING THE RIGHT BED

A lot of people think that a comfortable bed should be as soft as possible. But this is simply not true. A soft bed 'gives' under the weight of the body, with the result that the spine spends the night in an awkward, curved position.

It is far better to sleep on a firm bed, which provides full support. Unfortunately, good quality beds are expensive: a cheap bed usually has relatively few springs and therefore sags all too easily, while a better quality one has more springs and therefore provides firmer support.

If you cannot afford to buy a good bed, try putting a board underneath the mattress. This is an effective compromise. Use $3/4$ inch blockboard or hardboard rather than chipboard, as these do not give so easily and are still relatively inexpensive. Ideally, the board should be as wide and as long as the mattress. In a double bed, this may mean putting two boards, side by side, under the mattress.

Different beds suit different people according to their weight. A 100kg (220lb) man will obviously benefit from a firmer bed than a 50kg (110lb) woman.

Do not be fooled by the term 'orthopaedic'. It implies some sort of medical approval but it is actually unlikely to have any. You may simply be paying more for the word!

Sleep as flat as possible, either on your side in a foetal position or on your back, and do not use more than one pillow. Any more will tend to have the effect of bending the lower spine. There are also specially designed pillows, which have a thin strip down the centre so they resemble the shape of a butterfly. These allow the neck to lie in line with the rest of the body.

MAKING THE BED

The main problem when making the bed is moving the mattress, which can make it difficult to tuck in the bedclothes. If you are replacing your mattress, buy a lightweight one which will make this easier. Continental quilts make bed making a lot easier, as well as being both warm and lightweight.

Another thing that makes bed making easier is to fit small blocks between the mattress and the bed to allow you to tuck in the bed-clothes.

CHAIRS

A lot of people think that a comfortable, easy chair is a deep, soft one. In fact, this sort of chair is probably responsible for a lot of back problems. It puts great strain on the spine, not least when you try to get up out of it and is never a good idea for someone who suffers from any sort of backache. In addition, too low a chair can give you problems unbending stiff knees when you get up.

An upright chair, which provides good support for the lower spine, is far more protective. Arm rests and a head rest provide extra support. A foot rest may also help. If your chair does not provide you with adequate support in the small of the back, try putting a small cushion that fits snugly there. Change your position often so as to avoid getting stiff in any of your joints.

Office chairs are particularly important for anyone who spends all day sitting at a desk. A lot more attention is paid these days to the design of office chairs and to their relation to the corresponding work surface. It is worth making sure that yours suits you (*see Chapter 8*).

DRIVING

A lot of arthritis sufferers find it both uncomfortable and tiring to drive any great distance. That does not mean to say, however, that you will have to give up driving a car. Cars, in fact, can make life a lot easier than struggling about on public transport.

If you're thinking of buying a new car, try it out for as long as you can before coming to any decision. Many car seats, particularly those in small cars, can be blamed for causing backaches. The best car seats are shaped to fit the hollow of the back and can be adjusted in both the height and the angle of back rest. The best ones also have integral neck restraints.

If you can afford the luxuries of power steering and an automatic gearbox, these will also lighten the experience of driving. If you find it difficult to operate the door handles or controls, speak to an occupational therapist, who may be able to help you find solutions to the problem. Your local garage may be able to help, too. Don't forget that if you have any alterations done to your car, you should inform your insurance company.

POSTURE

Good posture is particularly important for the arthritis sufferer. You should:

- stand upright;
- hold your head up;
- keep your back straight;
- keep your shoulders relaxed;
- tuck in your bottom and tummy;
- balance your weight equally on both feet.

If you find it difficult to stand for long periods of time, don't. This is not giving in, it is just being sensible. You may find it a good idea to carry a perching stool or shooting-stick around with you so that you don't have to stand for too long.

KEEPING WARM

People with arthritis tend to move slowly and, especially if they are also getting on in years, are in danger of becoming too cold. If they are outside, they may not even be aware of how cold they are getting. It has even been known, in extreme cases, for someone to develop hypothermia and to collapse and become unable to move their limbs.

This is rare but anyone who suffers from arthritis should be aware of the possibility and should not stay out in the cold for too long. Always wear several layers of warm clothing, and if you feel tired or even lightheaded, get yourself into the warm as quickly as you can. Ideally, get into bed, where you stand the best and quickest chance of conserving your own heat and reestablishing control of your metabolism. Stay there until you have warmed up.

Invest in a warm dressing-gown, and keep your extremities warm with gloves and bedsocks. If you like fresh air in your bedroom at night, you may also like a woolly hat to prevent yourself losing heat through your head – we all lose about a third of our body heat in this way. A bed jacket or a shawl is also useful for when you are sitting up in bed.

HEAT

Heat is acknowledged as providing many sufferers with relief. If you benefit from heat, you will probably benefit from starting the day with a warm bath. How to apply heat depends on which part of the body is affected. A stiff neck, for example, is often helped simply by a warm scarf. Painful hands may benefit from soaking in a bowl of warm water. The easiest way of applying heat virtually anywhere is with a hotwater bottle. Sitting in front of a radiant electric fire can also help. In both these cases, however, it is obviously always important to be careful not to burn the skin.

Warm wax baths can be highly beneficial to the painful hand. A special grade of paraffin wax should be used for this purpose, which is available from the chemist. It is important to use the right kind of wax, as the wrong sort could badly burn the skin, so be sure to tell the chemist what you want it for.

The wax is gently melted in a double saucepan (not directly over heat), being careful not to overheat it, until it has just melted. The hand is then dipped in and out of the wax about six times until it is covered in a thick coating of warm wax. It is then wrapped in cotton wool and bandages, which act to preserve the heat. Leave the hand in its wax coating for at least half an hour. It is possible to move the joints during this time while the hand is inside its wax coating. At the end of the treatment time, strip off the wax and put it to one side for remelting.

A heat lamp can also bring temporary relief to a painful joint, but its effects are usually short-lived, in which case buying it could be a waste of money. Ask your doctor's advice. He may refer you to a physiotherapist who will consider various forms of pain relief, including heat. If a heat lamp works for you, it may be worth buying your own, but be careful always to use it at least 18 inches away from the joint and not to use it for more than about 20 minutes at a time.

EPSOM SALTS BATH

Many people with arthritis report the use of Epsom salts in the bath water as being very therapeutic. One explanation for this is that Epsom salts may act as a drawing agent for acid in the body, which some people believe plays an important part in the development of arthritis. Epsom salts are available from chemists.

Simply add three teacupfuls of Epsom salts in a warm bath. Do not use any other bath additive, such as bath salts or oils, as their alkalinity would interfere with the action of the Epsom salts. Keep the water hot by adding more as you need it, and exercise painful joints in the bath. Stay in the bath for 10 to 15 minutes, then get out and dry yourself with a warm towel.

The best time to take an Epsom salts bath is just before bedtime when you can get straight into a warm bed. This will help keep the pores of the skin open and encourage sweating, which will continue the elimination of acid. Have a quick shower in the morning to rinse off the accumulated acids on your skin.

If you are unable to get into the bath, bathe the hands and feet in a kitchen bowl to which you have added one cupful of Epsom salts and soak for 10 to 15 minutes, while exercising the joints as much as you can. Do this several times a day and you should find that regular treatment will work wonders in just a few weeks, or if your condition is really bad in a few months.

GINGER BATH

Another special bath that some sufferers have found beneficial is a ginger bath. This is reputed to be particularly good for pains in the legs, ankles, knees and hips, as well as for a lower backache.

To prepare this, slice 450g (1lb) of fresh ginger root into small pieces. Place these in a cotton sack or pillowcase, or tie them up in a piece of cheesecloth, and boil in about 8 litres (2 gallons) of water for an hour or so.

Put the cooking water in the bath and soak in it until the water begins to cool.

COLD

Heat does not work for everyone, though. Some people actually find that their painful joints react better to cold, in which case they may prefer to soak their hands in cold water, or to use an ice-pack on painful joints. A packet of frozen peas wrapped in a towel makes a good makeshift ice-pack.

A cold compress can ease inflammation and pain. Wring out a piece of linen, or similar fabric, in cold water. Wrap this around the affected joint and cover it with some warm, woollen fabric. This will increase circulation to the affected area and can have a near miraculous effect.

CLIMATE

One commonly held view is that it is inclement weather, and in particular cold, damp weather, that causes arthritis. Indeed, many sufferers claim they can forecast such weather changes by the state of their rheumatic pains. Pain in the joints does seem to be particularly sensitive to changes in weather conditions but, so far, no one is sure why this should be so.

Eager to find the truth about the link between weather and arthritis, researchers have done a lot of work on the subject. They have looked, for example, at conditions in Jamaica. Jamaica is known for its wonderful climate, yet there is virtually the same incidence of arthritis there as in Britain.

That said, though, the pain felt was generally less severe. So although cold, damp weather is not responsible for the onset of arthritis, and although hot sunny weather will not prevent it, it does seem that warm sunny weather may ease the pain.

Given the role played by heat in pain relief, this is hardly surprising. Sensible sunbathing, and that means not overdoing it, can therefore be highly beneficial. But be mindful of the warnings and sunbathe in the early morning and late afternoon when the sun is not too high or too hot, rather than when the rays are at their most damaging in terms of sunburn and skin cancers.

Warm weather does not suit everyone, however. Some people actually feel better in cold weather. You should adjust your home temperature according to which temperature suits you best.

You should hesitate before doing anything as drastic as moving simply because you think a different climate might suit you better. For one thing, it might not actually help, and for another, you run the risk of cutting yourself off from family and friends, whose company and support may be of great importance to you when you are not feeling well.

PLAN AHEAD

It is important to avoid getting overtired and this means planning ahead. Be organised about how you spend your time. Are there things that someone else can do for you, or things that don't need doing at all? Do only the things that have to be done and that you really want to do. Good planning saves time, conserves energy and allows you to do things more efficiently and less painfully.

Don't be frightened to ask other people to help you. The chances are they'll be only too pleased to help; they just didn't want to 'interfere' and they need to be told exactly what you would like them to do.

LABOUR-SAVING DEVICES

You need every labour-saving device you can afford. A washing machine is invaluable, a dishwasher is a great help, and a microwave oven means no more heavy saucepans or hot heavy dishes to handle from the oven, and no more burnt-on pans to scrub.

CLOTHES

You can make life easier for yourself by wearing loose fitting, comfortable clothes that are easy to fasten and unfasten, and to slip on and off. Zips are easier to handle than buttons, and Velcro fastenings are easier than press-studs. Cardigans are easier than jumpers.

Above all, do not wear anything that aggravates your arthritis and that includes shoes. High fashion is simply not important enough to make you endure pain – it's just not worth it.

SHOES

Choose shoes that give your feet good support, preferably with plenty of cushioning in the sole. If this is a problem, a chiropodist can fit you with special inner soles.

Shoes should also be easy to get on and off. Avoid shoes that are too tight around the toes. Similarly, tights and socks should not be tight around the toes.

The soles should be flexible and non-slip. The uppers should be soft and supple, preferably without seams, which can put pressure on the toes.

Avoid high heeled shoes, which push the weight forward and put too much pressure on the ball of the foot and the toes. The load on the foot should be equally spread between the ball of the foot and the heel. If you really want to wear a heel, choose as low a one as possible. Fashion is not so averse to this kind of shoe these days and it is easy to find shoes that both feel and look good.

A regular visit to a chiropodist, who can deal with existing problems and help prevent future ones, is invaluable.

When feet are swollen and painful, rest them. Putting your feet up – literally – will help ease the swelling. Then, when both swelling and pain have subsided, exercise them (*see Chapter 4*).

BODY CARE

People don't realise until it affects them, but arthritis can make many of those little things that you do every day of your life surprisingly awkward.

Combing the hair can become a painful business, so choose an easy-care hairstyle and use a lightweight comb or brush that passes easily through the hair. A long-handled comb or brush will allow you to attend to the back of your hair without straining painful shoulders. Washing the hair can be an even greater problem, so go to the hairdresser if you can afford it or ask a friend or relative to help you.

Use whatever helps you when applying make-up. A cosmetic sponge makes it easier to apply foundation, as it lessens the strain on the fingers. Choose cosmetics that come in lightweight containers that are easy to open and close. On the whole, it's best to avoid tubes, which can be very difficult to handle.

If you can, sit rather than stand to wash, and shower rather than bathe. Make sure there is a non-slip surface on the bottom of the bath, and if there isn't, use a special purpose rubber bath mat.

It's generally better to use a sponge than a flannel because it's easier to get the excess water out of it, using the palm of the hand or the forearm. If you find it particularly difficult to wash the neck, back, legs or feet, a loofah with straps at the ends may help, or you may like to buy a specially long piece of flannelling, with plastic loops at either end, from the chemist which will ease this problem. Similarly, you can attach loops to either end of a long, narrow piece of towelling to dry parts of the body that are difficult to reach, such as your back and feet.

You may find it difficult to hold a wet bar of soap, in which case it may be easier to use liquid soap or 'soap on a rope'. Lever taps are easier than knob taps, and a damp cloth will help increase your grip on either.

Similarly, a rubber band wound round the handle of your toothbrush will increase your grip. Alternatively, you may find it easier to use an electric toothbrush.

Shaving can be difficult for any man who has stiff wrists or hands, in which case a lightweight disposable razor may be the answer. It may be difficult to use a brush and soap, in which case it may be easier to apply lather to the face with an aerosol foam. A shelf positioned at the right height for you will help you to rest your arm while shaving.

SMOKING

There are many reasons for not smoking and most people are only too familiar with these. No one should smoke and this applies in particular to people suffering from arthritis.

A smoker loses up to 15 per cent of the oxygen in his or her blood. This means that less oxygen is circulating round the body and that any damage or pains may be even worse than they otherwise would.

Smoking is known to deplete the body of certain vitamins, notably vitamin C, which is so essential to the maintenance of good health. Given the importance for anyone with arthritis of following a wholesome diet (*see Chapter 5*), it is particularly foolish to spoil all the good work by smoking.

FISH OIL SUPPLEMENTS

Recent research has suggested that fish oils, such as cod liver oil, may have an anti-inflammatory effect and may therefore be beneficial to arthritics. This has not been scientifically proven but many sufferers are convinced that fish oil supplements help them.

So if you feel better as a result of taking your preferred fish oil supplement, carry on taking it. If it does not seem to be helping after a couple of months, you might consider stopping although fish oil is known to have a long-term health benefit in the prevention of heart disease and, as such, it is probably worth taking anyway. You may be killing two birds with one stone.

COPPER BRACELETS

A lot of people swear by copper bracelets, convinced that they actually ease the pain of arthritis. The idea behind wearing them is that the absorption of copper through the skin may have a beneficial effect. There is no scientific evidence to support this and it remains unclear whether it is an old wives' tale or a wise bit of folklore.

That said, though, a lot of people are convinced they work and they certainly won't do you any harm. If you want to wear one, do.

Many people have their own version of a magic talisman to ward off disease, or to prevent it getting any worse. There are all sorts of strange tales, including those of people who carry nutmegs or new potatoes in their pockets to keep away disease. Copper bracelets are no odder!

BEE VENOM

One 'remedy' that is undoubtedly odder is that of bee venom. There are people who believe that being stung by a bee provides instant relief from arthritic pain, though there are also others, as with most 'cures', who are quick to dispute this view.

There is a bee-keeper in Vermont who has given free treatments with live bee stings for over 50 years to people with arthritis. There are also doctors in America who administer bee venom through a hypodermic needle.

Whatever you do, though, do not encourage bees to sting you. It is possible, if not very common, to be allergic to bee venom, an allergy that can, in extreme cases, be fatal.

HERBAL REMEDIES

Some herbal remedies, such as greenlipped mussel extract, are popular with aficionados, though there is little evidence that they actually do anything to cure arthritis. Although they are usually not toxic, like any drug they can sometimes cause side-effects, such as insomnia, irritability and ironically, as they are the very thing they are intended to prevent, joint pains (*see Chapter 6*).

ACUPRESSURE

Rubbing the part that hurts is a natural instinct. It may, in fact, be the oldest form of physical therapy there is.

Acupressure has a lot in common with acupuncture (*see Chapter 6*), in which fine needles are inserted into the skin, according to a network of points in the body that have a proven beneficial effect. The advantage of acupressure, which uses finger pressure rather than needles, is that you can do it yourself.

One way of finding an acupressure point is to massage, quite firmly, the area that hurts. Soreness under pressure suggests some kind of blockage in the circulation surrounding that point. Then, when you have found the place that seems most directly related to your pain, hold it gently but firmly using your middle finger, which is the longest and strongest of your fingers, with the index and ring fingers on either side to provide support, for between three and five minutes.

Start applying pressure slowly and, similarly, release it slowly. The degree of pressure you need to apply varies from one person and perhaps one joint to another. If it hurts a lot, apply touch rather than pressure. Even this can be effective in relieving pain and inflammation. If your hand is too painful or too weak to apply the required finger pressure, use the knuckles of your fist or try using some sort of aid, such as a golf ball or an avocado stone.

Do this for up to 15 minutes in all, two or three times a day say, morning, lunch time and before you go to bed. You will obtain the maximum benefit from acupressure if you follow each session with deep relaxation. Best of all, take a nap, even if it is for only a few minutes. This will have the effect of encouraging your joints to heal and strengthen.

OILS, CREAMS AND RUBS

There are many creams, lotions, balms and liniments advertised as providing relief for arthritis. They are easily available from health food shops and chemists.

Some of them seem to be of particular benefit to some sufferers who have not found relief in any other way. Some people find rubs to be especially helpful at certain times, such as before bedtime, or immediately before or after exercising.

Two that should work are ibuprofen (Ibuleve) gel which is available over the counter from your chemist and fenbrufen (Traxam) available on prescription only – test either first for possible adverse skin reaction.

Some people swear by oils of rosemary and juniper, mixed together in equal amounts and rubbed onto arthritic joints. This is said to be especially good for the relief of backache.

Another oil that is said to be good for reducing joint inflammation and easing painful joints is peanut oil. Warm it gently before use.

KEEPING A DIARY

It is useful to keep a log of any changes that have occurred in your condition and link them with what else has been going on in your life. In this way you may be able to establish a pattern of activities and events which will enable you to avoid things that exacerbate your condition, and to apply those things that relieve it. Fill in the following diary on a weekly basis for at least three months.

1. Would you describe your condition as:
   - ☐ aching?
   - ☐ painful?
   - ☐ stiff?
   - ☐ tense?
   - ☐ tired?
2. Is the pain:
   - ☐ sharp?
   - ☐ dull?

3. Is the pain:
☐ constant? ☐ intermittent?
4. Is it worse:
☐ in the morning? ☐ during the day?
☐ at work? ☐ before you go to sleep?
5. Which area of your body hurts most?
☐ arms ☐ elbows
☐ wrists ☐ hands
☐ fingers ☐ legs
☐ knees ☐ ankles
☐ feet ☐ toes
☐ hips ☐ upper back
☐ lower back ☐ small of the back
☐ neck
6. What makes your arthritis worse?
☐ standing ☐ sitting
☐ lying down ☐ driving
☐ cold weather ☐ wet weather
☐ menstruating ☐ stress
☐ other
7. What is most badly affected?
☐ sleep ☐ appetite
☐ breathing ☐ toilet habits
☐ work ☐ sex life
☐ morale
8. What helps relieve your pain?
☐ rest ☐ exercise
☐ relaxation ☐ diet
☐ other
9. Comments:

CONCLUDING REMARKS

We have dealt in some detail in this chapter with ways of alleviating pain in the short term. Not everything will work for the same person, but it is to be hoped that some of it will work for you.

In the next three chapters, we shall be focusing on your life-style and on things you can do to improve the quality of your life. It is by making such judicious changes in your life that you may hope to achieve lasting relief.

4 Exercises That Work

There are a number of exercises that you can do at home and that many people with arthritis have found to be beneficial. What follows is a number of these, grouped under particular parts of the body.

The aim of these exercises is:

- to maintain the full range of body movement;
- to prevent deformities;
- to keep muscles strong.

Try them. If they hurt, stop and try again another day. It is important not to allow your joints to get stuck or your muscles to waste, so these exercises are vital. It is better to do a little too much than to do a lot too little or, even worse, nothing at all. However, take care not to go through your own pain threshold – any unusual twinges or pains signify that it's time to rest.

The rule is to do regular exercises to help you attain maximum joint flexibility and muscle strength. If they make you feel in any way better – and that may mean your joints being both less stiff and less painful – make them part of your daily routine.

The following exercises are all quite simple and you should be able to do them without any problem. If, however, they prove too difficult or you feel you need more specialised advice, you would probably benefit from the advice of a qualified physiotherapist.

Physiotherapy entails exercising under supervision, with the aid of weights, benches and bars, slings suspended from the ceiling, frames, chairs and stands. It won't actually cure your arthritis, but it undoubtedly does much to improve both the power and tone of your muscles and the flexibility of your joints – all of which means you will find it much easier and less painful to move around.

BREATHING EXERCISES

Everyone should do some deep-breathing exercises several times a day – preferably in the open air but at least at an open window. These will relieve tension, make you feel more relaxed, improve circulation, exercise your lungs and stop you feeling sluggish, and will generally make you feel calmer and more at ease, with both yourself and the world.

The exercises should be done smoothly and continuously, never holding the breath or stopping at any point.

1. Stand naturally, with your arms loosely by your side.
2. Keeping your mouth closed, take a deep breath through both nostrils, filling your lungs to full capacity.
3. Now breathe out completely, letting all the air out of your lungs.
4. Repeat ten times.
5. Now do the same things, but breathing through one nostril at a time while you press the other one closed with a finger.

LIMBERING-UP EXERCISES

Before you start, it is important for everyone to do a set of limbering-up exercises. They are best done first thing in the morning, perhaps after getting out of bed and before getting dressed. If you are very stiff in the morning, a warm shower or bath – or perhaps just taking a foot or hand bath, depending on where you are stiff – should help considerably. You will then be ready to face the day.

It's easiest to do the following exercises sitting down, and work from your feet upwards.

1. Working on one ankle at a time, move it up and down. Do this ten times on each ankle.

2. Working on one ankle at a time, move it around in as full a circle as possible. Do five clockwise rotations and five anti-clockwise rotations on each ankle.
3. Bend your knees as much as you can, then straighten them out fully. Do this ten times.
4. Roll your head gently from side to side. Repeat ten times.

SPECIFIC EXERCISES

Exactly which exercises you need to do – and indeed which ones you are able to do – depends largely on your particular condition and on which joints are affected. Here are some exercises that can help prevent the shoulders, neck, back, hips, knees, ankles, feet, wrists and hands from becoming rigid, weak and painful.

SHOULDERS

The shoulders are a distressingly common place for stiffness and pain.

Arm swings
1. Sit up straight on an upright chair with no arms or on a stool.
2. Let both arms hang down on either side of you.
3. Swing one arm forwards and backwards in a slow, continuous movement.
4. Repeat with the other arm.
5. Repeat with both arms simultaneously.

Outward swings
1. Sit up straight on an upright chair with no arms or on a stool.
2. Let both arms hang down on either side of you.
3. Swing one arm outwards at a right angle away from your body.
4. Repeat with the other arm.

5. Repeat with both arms simultaneously.
6. Repeat the entire sequence five times.

Shoulder shrugs
1. Sit up straight on an upright chair.
2. Shrug your shoulders up to your ears.
3. Slowly lower your shoulders again.
4. Repeat ten times.

Reaching for back of head
1. Sit up straight on an upright chair with no arms or on a stool.
2. Lift one arm up to put the hand at the back of the head as if you were combing the back of your hair.
3. Repeat with the other arm.
4. Repeat with both arms simultaneously.
5. Repeat the entire sequence five times.

Reaching for shoulder blades
1. Sit up straight on an upright chair with no arms or on a stool.
2. Place one hand behind the back and try to reach up to touch the shoulder blade on the same side. You may not be able to achieve this fully – do what you can within the limits of your own ability.
3. Repeat with the other hand.
4. Repeat five times on each side.

Rotating the shoulders
1. Sit up straight on an upright chair with no arms or on a stool.
2. Lift and rotate one shoulder.
3. Lift and rotate the other shoulder.
4. Lift and rotate both shoulders together.
5. Repeat the entire sequence five times.

Shoulder touch
1. Stand upright.

2. Touch each shoulder with the fingertips of each same-arm hand.
3. Then stretch both arms forward.
4. Touch each shoulder with the fingertips of each same-arm hand again.
5. Then stretch both arms sideways.
6. Repeat the entire sequence five to ten times.

NECK

Arthritis often settles in the neck joints, where it can cause a lot of pain. This pain can then radiate to the head, face and shoulders. The following exercises will stretch and loosen up tightness in the neck muscles, as well as improving general circulation.

Sideways bends
1. Sit up straight in an upright chair.
2. Bend the neck slowly to one side, trying to touch the shoulder with the ear.
3. Repeat with the other side.
4. Repeat five to ten times on both sides.

Forward bends
1. Sit up straight in an upright chair.
2. Let your head drop forwards, trying to touch your chest with your chin. Do not force it.
3. Lift the head upwards again.
4. Repeat five to ten times.

Neck rotations
1. Sit up straight in an upright chair.
2. Slowly rotate the neck to one side, as if you were trying to look behind you.
3. Repeat on the other side.
4. Repeat five times.

BACK

A stiff, painful back can be all pervasive and can seem to take all the joy out of life. The following exercises should be practised every day, unless your back is actually too painful.

Back bends
1. Stand up straight.
2. Bend forwards as far as you can towards your toes.
3. Straighten up.
4. Now lean backwards and look up towards the ceiling.
5. Repeat the entire sequence, in a gentle, continuous movement. Repeat five to ten times.

Sideways bends
1. Stand up straight, with your feet a shoulder width apart.
2. Bend slowly sideways to the left, moving your left hand down the side of your left thigh.
3. Straighten up.
4. Repeat to the right.
5. Repeat five to ten times on each side.

Spine rotations
1. Stand up straight, with your feet a comfortable distance apart and your toes pointing straight in front of you.
2. Put your hands on your hips and rotate your spine to the left, without moving your feet. Hold for a count of ten.
3. Rotate your spine back to the centre.
4. Repeat to the right-hand side.
5. Repeat the entire sequence ten times.

Head raise
1. Lie flat on your back on the floor.
2. Press the head and shoulder as hard as you can into the floor.
3. Using your stomach muscles, lift your head up to look at your toes.

4.   Lower your head to the floor.
5.   Repeat ten times.

HIPS

A painful hip is one of the most common problems experienced by people who have osteoarthritis, and also one of the most debilitating. There are several simple exercises that should help make it more flexible and easier for you to walk. The main thing is to rotate the hip joint so that the capsule around it does not contract or seize up.

If your hips are stiff, these movements will be somewhat restricted. Regular exercises should make them easier, however, as the range of movement increases.

Sideways swing
1.   Stand behind an upright chair, holding the back as a support.
2.   Swing out the leg on the affected side at a right angle to your body. Move it as far as you can, without it causing you pain.
3.   Meanwhile, keep the other leg as straight as you can, and hold your body upright. Do not allow your body to lean away from the leg you are swinging out. If you do this, your good hip will take all the strain and the bad one will not move at all, which of course makes it much easier but also defeats the whole point of the exercise.

Forward swing
1.   Stand to one side of an upright chair, holding the back as a support.
2.   Swing the leg on the affected side forwards and backwards.
3.   Meanwhile, keep the other leg as straight as you can, and hold your body upright. Do not allow your body to lean in any direction – backwards, forwards or sideways.

Leg sequence

1. Lie on your back on the floor, with your legs straight and your feet a comfortable distance apart.
2. Bend your left knee up towards your chest. Use both hands to pull your knee gently but firmly towards you. Hold for a few seconds.
3. Slowly put your leg back on the floor and stretch it out straight again.
4. Repeat with the right leg.
5. Now lift up your left leg, keeping the knee as straight as you can. You may not be able to left it very high at first, but it is more important to keep the knee straight. Hold for a count of ten.
6. Slowly lower the leg to the floor.
7. Repeat with the right leg.
8. Keeping your heels together, bend both knees up towards your chest and then part them outwards as far as they will go. Hold for a count of ten.
9. Now bring your knees together and slowly lower your legs to the floor.
10. Lift up your left leg, keeping the knee as straight as you can, and move it gently to the side, taking it as far as you can. Hold for a count of ten.
11. Now move the leg back to the centre and slowly lower it to the floor.
12. Repeat with the right leg.

Sideways leg raises

1. Lie on your left-hand side on the floor, with both legs as straight as possible.
2. Keeping both legs straight and putting your right hand on the floor in front of you for support, lift your right leg up in the air about 20cm (12 inches). Hold for a few seconds.
3. Bring the leg down slowly onto the other one.
4. Repeat five times.

5. Turn over and repeat five times with the other leg.

WAIST

The waist area can lose a lot of its mobility. The following exercise will help retrieve some of this flexibility.

Waist swiveller

1. Sit up straight in an upright chair, with your arms hanging down on either side of the chair.
2. Now swivel the top half of your body round to the left-hand side, moving your left arm over the back of the chair and placing your right hand over your left thigh.
3. Swivel round to the right-hand side, moving your right arm over the back of the chair and placing your left hand over your right thigh.

KNEES

It is most important to keep the thigh muscles strong and to avoid the knees becoming stuck in a bent position.

Knee straightening

1. Sit in an upright chair. Alternatively, this exercise can be done in bed.
2. Straighten the leg fully and try to push your knee gently very slightly backwards. You should feel the thigh muscles tighten. Hold for a count of ten.
3. Repeat 10 or 20 times for each knee.

Knees out

1. Lie on the floor on your back.
2. With your legs stretched out in front of you, slide your feet back towards your bottom, so that your knees are bent.
3. Swing each knee outwards, keeping the movement slow and gentle. Do not jerk.

4. Swing the knees inwards again, bringing them back together.
5. Repeat ten times and gradually increase to 20.

ANKLES

A lot of people – whether they have arthritis or not – suffer from very stiff ankles. The following exercise, done regularly, should help remedy this.

Heel and toe
1. Sit up straight in an upright chair.
2. Keeping both feet on the ground, lift up the heel of the left foot so that the ball of the foot is almost vertical. Hold for a few seconds.
3. Then lift up the toes of the left foot and hold for a few seconds.
4. Repeat with the right foot.
5. Repeat with both feet together.
6. Repeat the whole sequence five to ten times.

FEET

Your feet support you for an entire lifetime. They therefore deserve to be well looked after.

Push and pump
1. Lie on your back with your legs stretched out in front of you.
2. Raise the legs onto pillows.
3. Put your left foot through a pedalling motion, and then do the same with the right. You should be particularly careful to push right down each time, making the calf muscles work strongly to produce a good pumping action, as this will help to drain fluid out of the feet and legs.

4. Do this for five minutes, after which time you should leave the legs raised for half an hour or so.

TOES

The toes can be very badly affected by arthritis. Toe exercises do much to improve circulation, to tone up weak muscles and to encourage greater flexibility.

Pencil exercise
1. While you are standing up, slowly grasp a pencil horizontally with your toes, so that your toes curl round the pencil.
2. Release and repeat ten times for each foot.

Tip-toes
1. While you are standing up, rise up and down on your toes.
2. Repeat ten times.

WRISTS

Wrists are an often neglected area and benefit greatly from a little exercise.

Wrist rotations
1. Sit on an upright chair.
2. Rotate one of your wrists right round, first in one direction and then in the other.
3. Repeat with the other wrist.
4. Repeat with both wrists simultaneously.

HANDS

Hands may be only a small part of the body, but stiff, painful fingers are a surprisingly big problem. Exercises will do a lot to keep them more nimble.

Fingers walk
1. Place the hands palms downwards on a table.

2. 'Walk' the fingers across from little finger to thumb, while flattening the fingers and wrists as much as possible.
3. Bend your fingers tightly into a ball.
4. Stretch the fingers out fully.
5. Repeat the whole sequence five or ten times.

Fingers and thumbs

1. Sit with the palms uppermost.
2. Work on one hand at a time. Take the thumb across to the tip of the little finger.
3. Move the thumb down to the base of the little finger.
4. Repeat with each finger.
5. Repeat with the other hand.

AN EXERCISE PROGRAMME

You can select from these exercises a varied programme that suits your particular needs and abilities. Do not concentrate on only one exercise to the exclusion of all others for more than a few minutes.

Aim, at the start, to exercise for 10 minutes each day, ideally at the start of the day. Gradually build up to 20-30 minutes a day. Do not push yourself too hard. You will achieve better results if you follow a gentle but regular programme.

You will soon be astounded at your improved mobility and strength. With this will come an enhanced sense of well-being.

5 Eat What Works

The effect of diet on arthritis remains the subject of much controversy. There are many questions concerning diet that every sufferer from arthritis asks: Is there a special diet I can follow? Are there any miracle foods I should add to my shopping list? Should I avoid certain foods? Should I eat less? Or more?

And unfortunately, the answers to these questions are not always straightforward. Given that there are so many different forms of arthritis as well as so many different types of food, this is probably hardly surprising.

There are, however, certain basic principles that should help you develop your own guidelines.

NO PROOF

Many different diets have been developed over the years, by both sufferers and their doctors. The people who have devised these diets always swear by them, as the only way of combating this painful disease. But none of them has ever been able to prove it.

That said, though, many doctors are prepared to accept that there may be some link between diet and arthritis. It is possible that, in some sufferers, there may be a genuine relationship between certain foods and brief episodes of joint pain.

The problem is that what works for one person may not work for another. What evidence there is tends to be no more than anecdotal, which means you must compile your own evidence and follow what suits you.

If you wish to experiment with your diet, then there's no reason why you shouldn't. The only provisos are that the diet you follow is a safe one, and that it is not too expensive in terms of either time, money or effort. Any major change in diet should always be supervised by a doctor or dietitian, who will check that you are getting all the necessary components for good health.

There are literally dozens of different diets that people have devised. All too often they contradict each other widely, resulting in a confusing array of contradictory recommendations and prohibitions.

The dietary connection is not a simple matter. But patients suffering from arthritis often feel helpless, abandoned by the rest of the world to their painful fate. Changing diet is a relatively easy thing to do and gives patients the feeling that they are doing something to help themselves, that they are in control of their lives. For some people, this has enormous psychological benefits. It is almost as important, more so perhaps, than whether it works or not.

And if you find a diet that suits you, stick to it. Many sufferers think that, having followed a particular diet for a while and feeling so much better as a result, it might be all right now to break that diet once in a while. But this is not sensible. If it works, breaking it is likely to set you back straight away.

What follows is a look at some of the principal diets that have been suggested by various people.

DR COLLIN DONG'S DIET

Californian specialist Dr Collin Dong suffered badly from arthritis from the age of 35, which no amount of conventional drugs seemed to help. Yet, contrary to all expectations from orthodox doctors, he succeeded in curing himself by dietary means.

Dr Dong recalls his father saying to all his nine children whenever they became ill: "Bing chung how yup, woh chung how chu". Literally translated this means "Sickness enters through the mouth, and catastrophe comes out of the mouth".

Dr Dong recalls how this sage folk observation changed his life. "Incredible as it may sound, this axiom was the straw (at which I was grasping) that eventually rescued me from a wheelchair. This old adage pointed me in another direction. Perhaps I had been putting some 'sickness' through my mouth for a long time without realising it."

And so was born Dr Dong's allergy theory of arthritis and his nutritional approach, based on wholefoods and no artificial additives, that he and many of his followers have found so successful. His diet is far removed from the modern predilection for processed, convenience and junk foods but thousands of sufferers who have followed his diet have found it to be nothing short of a miracle cure.

It's a very strict diet and not at all easy to follow, but well worth the dedication it demands if it works for you.

Permitted foods

- ☐ fish
- ☐ fresh vegetables
- ☐ margarine free of milk solids
- ☐ honey
- ☐ sunflower seeds
- ☐ rice of all kinds
- ☐ crispbreads
- ☐ garlic
- ☐ sugar in moderation
- ☐ tea

- ☐ seafood
- ☐ vegetable oils
- ☐ egg whites

- ☐ nuts
- ☐ soya bean products
- ☐ wholemeal bread
- ☐ onions
- ☐ flour of all kinds
- ☐ salt
- ☐ decaffeinated coffee

Forbidden foods

- ☐ meat (except breast of chicken occasionally)
- ☐ all fruit
- ☐ tomatoes
- ☐ butter
- ☐ yoghurt

- ☐ fruit juices
- ☐ milk
- ☐ cheese
- ☐ egg yolks

☐ vinegar   ☐ pepper
☐ chocolate
☐ dry roasted nuts (the process involves monosodium glutamate)
☐ alcohol (except occasionally a small amount of wine in
cooking)
☐ any food containing chemical additives, especially monosodium glutamate

DR JARVIS'S DIET

Dr Jarvis of Vermont, another famous doctor, recommends a quite
different course of action. Thousands of people have followed his
recommendations and many of them have reported great success.

Recommendations

Dr Jarvis advises taking the following 'cocktail', to be sipped with
every meal. It consists of:

- 2 teaspoonfuls of cider vinegar
- 2 teaspoonfuls of honey
- a glass of water

Three times a week, you add a drop of iodine to the honey and
vinegar mixture at one of your meals. In addition, you take one kelp
tablet every morning with your breakfast. Kelp is made from seaweed
and is said to contain a perfectly balanced combination of more than
60 minerals or trace elements, over 12 vitamins, and 21 amino acids.

Forbidden foods

☐ wheat breads   ☐ wheat cakes
☐ wheat cereals   ☐ white sugar
☐ citrus fruits and   ☐ beef
fruit juices
☐ lamb   ☐ pork

DR GIRAUD CAMPBELL'S DIET

Yet another American specialist, Dr Campbell, promises total pain relief in a matter of weeks, and the complete restoration of damaged bone structure in a matter of months.

His diet begins with a fast, and works up to the complete range of foods in a month or so.

Permitted foods
- □ raw, organic fruit
- □ fresh milk
- □ free-range eggs
- □ raw, organic vegetables
- □ lean meats
- □ natural cheese
- □ fresh fish

Forbidden foods
- □ tea
- □ soft drinks
- □ bread
- □ all canned foods
- □ ice-cream
- □ coffee
- □ alcohol
- □ all flour products
- □ all processed foods
- □ sweets

DR MAX WARMBRAND'S DIET

Dr Warmbrand, one of America's best-known naturopathic physicians, believes in treating his patients naturally. He starts them off on a liquid fast, with water, fruit juices, hot vegetable broth or herb tea, for a few days in order to promote an intensive elimination of toxins. This is followed by strict adherence to a largely vegetarian diet, with plenty of raw vegetables and fruits.

Permitted foods
- □ nuts
- □ wholewheat bread
- □ 'cottage cheese
- □ lean fish
- □ fresh vegetables
- □ honey
- □ skimmed milk
- □ chicken

☐ sprouted seeds and legumes
☐ fresh fruits that are in season

Forbidden foods

☐ meat, especially beef   ☐ coffee
☐ tea   ☐ sugar
☐ cream   ☐ fatty cheeses
☐ cakes   ☐ pastries
☐ spicy foods   ☐ butter
☐ white bread and   ☐ refined and processed
    other white flour   cereals
    products

GENERAL GUIDELINES

In general, there is so much conflicting dietary advice relating to arthritis that it leaves the confused sufferer with two choices. Either, he or she plumps for one of the specific diets mentioned here (but it is necessary to read about it in greater detail and then to follow it to the letter), or he or she follows a set of general guidelines, which are given below.

The only rule is that there are no rules. No two sufferers are exactly the same and neither is their condition.

The guidelines given below include a lot of the general advice for healthy eating, plus a few more specific ones relating to arthritis.

- Eat less fat.
- Use low-fat cooking methods, such as steaming, baking, grilling, poaching and microwaving. Stirfry rather than fry.
- Don't skip breakfast.
- Learn to recognise your sensitivities to foods. These vary from one person to another. Common culprits include citrus fruits, chocolate, tomatoes, green peppers, aubergines.

- Read the labels on food to help you choose the items that are lowest in fat, salt, sugar, and highest in protein and carbohydrate.
- Drink plenty of water. Skimmed milk and fruit juices are also acceptable.
- Don't force yourself to eat any food that doesn't appeal to your tastes.
- Eat five or six small meals a day rather than three large ones. This allows your digestion to work efficiently and continuously without the strain of coping with too much bulk all at once.
- Chew your food well.
- Enjoy your food. It should be a very real and important pleasure in your life.

FOODS TO EAT:

- ☐ fresh fruit
- ☐ fresh vegetables
- ☐ when these are not available, frozen vegetables
- ☐ salads
- ☐ fresh fish, particularly fatty fish
- ☐ when it is not available, frozen fish
- ☐ shellfish
- ☐ poultry
- ☐ wholegrain breads and cereals
- ☐ dried beans and peas
- ☐ low-fat foods
- ☐ skimmed rather than full-fat milk
- ☐ low-fat polyunsaturated margarine rather than butter
- ☐ wholewheat pasta
- ☐ brown rice
- ☐ low-fat yoghurt
- ☐ herbs and spices rather than salt
- ☐ herb teas
- ☐ decaffeinated coffee

FOODS TO AVOID:

- ☐ red meats, particularly beef and pork
- ☐ smoked and processed meats
- ☐ fatty foods
- ☐ fried foods
- ☐ saturated fats, such as butter, palm oil and meat fat
- ☐ processed foods
- ☐ junk foods
- ☐ alcohol
- ☐ salt
- ☐ sugar
- ☐ sweets
- ☐ caffeine, as in coffee, tea and cola drinks
- ☐ dairy products
- ☐ vegetables in the nightshade family, which include tomatoes, white potatoes, aubergine and peppers
- ☐ highly processed starches, such as white bread, white flour and white rice
- ☐ foods containing chemical additives, such as colourings and preservatives
- ☐ acid-heavy foods such as vinegar and citrus fruits
- ☐ chocolate

A SENSIBLE DIET

This is a sensible diet anyway, of which doctors and nutritionists the world over would approve. There can be no guarantee that it will cure your arthritis or alleviate pain, but there can be no doubt either that your general state of health will be greatly enhanced.

VITAMINS AND MINERALS

It is well known that vitamins and minerals are absolutely essential for good health, whether you have arthritis or not. But the arthritis sufferer may need them more than most.

This is because arthritis can actually cause additional nutritional problems. There are several reasons for this. Firstly, the pain associated with arthritis can often interfere with both food shopping and cooking, and can therefore lead to a dramatic decrease in enthusiasm for all things culinary. Secondly, arthritis can lead to a decrease in appetite, often caused by the nausea brought on by medication. Thirdly, surgery can increase the need for certain nutrients, notably vitamins C and A, and iron. Fourthly, some arthritis drugs can have the side-effect of interfering with the absorption of certain nutrients, particularly vitamin C, copper, selenium, zinc and calcium. And lastly, though no less significantly, the disease itself, particularly rheumatoid arthritis, can interfere with the way your body absorbs nutrients from the foods you eat.

If you are at all worried about whether or not your diet is adequate and properly balanced, talk to your doctor or dietitian.

THE ROLE OF VITAMINS IN ARTHRITIS

Some vitamins are known to play specific roles in relieving certain problems caused by arthritis. For example:

- vitamin C helps with bruising;
- vitamin E has an anti-inflammatory action;
- vitamin B6 relieves some cases of a form of arthritis affecting the wrists and known as carpal tunnel syndrome.

FOOD SUPPLEMENTS

Most arthritis sufferers take some sort of vitamin supplement. A daily multi-vitamin supplement is the simplest way of filling any gaps in your diet.

If you know you have any particular vitamin deficiencies, you may need to remedy these with the relevant supplements. Doing this may actually help make you feel better.

As long as you're sensible about it and don't take more than the recommended dosage, there's certainly nothing wrong with trying your preferred supplement.

But you don't want to waste your money. So if, after a couple of months or so, a supplement doesn't seem to be helping at all, you might as well stop it.

ALLERGIES

The possibility that your arthritis may be caused by an allergy is a familiar idea, upheld by a few, though admittedly not many, specialists. The fact that a lot of people with arthritis seem to suffer a 'flare-up' after eating a particular food would seem to support this theory.

IDENTIFYING AN ALLERGY

There are several clinics that specialise in the detection and treatment of allergies, not only for arthritis but also for many other complaints such as migraine and asthma. They'll take a medical history and details about your symptoms and your present diet. You will then spend a week or so on a 'low-risk' diet of bland foods that are known to be unlikely allergens for arthritis. You may be surprised at the end of this time to find that you feel remarkably well, quite possibly better than you have done for months or even years! The next stage of the process is to add various other foods to your diet until your particular allergen (or allergens) has been established.

Testing can be done while you are a resident patient in one of these clinics, which is likely to be expensive, or you can attend the clinic for a number of consultations while following the prescribed diet at home. This will be much cheaper but also more difficult, because you will have to be very strict with yourself. Even the smallest nibble or sip of a forbidden food can throw the whole process off course.

KEEPING A FOOD DIARY

It is also possible to follow this plan of action yourself. The best way of doing this is to keep a food diary, noting exactly what you eat and drink (and that means everything!) and every occurrence of pain. Do this every day for a few weeks and see if you can find any connection between the two. If drinking wine on Saturday night, say, is always followed by excruciating pain on Sunday, the message would seem to be quite simple. Just stop drinking wine and see if you notice any improvement. Then reintroduce it and see if the problem comes back. If it does, it would suggest that there is an irrefutable connection.

A CAUTIONARY TALE

Research has been done on those people who have found dietary changes to be beneficial. The results have been surprising and would tend to support the cynical viewpoint.

In general, it has been found that if the food they have cut out is then reintroduced into their diet under a different guise, no allergic reaction can be detected. This suggests that the changes they reported were psychological rather than due to any real physical effect on their joints.

GOUT

Gout is one form of arthritis in which diet is definitely known to play an important part.

It is an established fact that gout is caused by crystals that accumulate in the joints and these, in turn, are caused by higher than normal levels of a substance known as uric acid. Uric acid is manufactured in two main ways.

Some of it results from normal cell turnover but, in some blood conditions, such as polycythaemia (too many red cells), and in certain skin conditions, such as psoriasis, the amount of cell turnover is greatly increased. This means that people with these conditions are especially likely to develop gout.

And some of it comes from 'purines' in food. Too much purine in the diet will increase the level of uric acid and will therefore increase the likelihood of an attack, so people who suffer from gout need to be particularly careful about what they eat and drink.

In general, the best advice they can follow is to avoid foods with a high purine content (*see table below*). There is some irony in this, in that oily fish like anchovies, herring and sardines, which can be so beneficial to people with other forms of arthritis, can actually worsen gout because of their high purine content. It's reassuring to know that other types of fish, however, contain no more purines than equivalent portions of meat or poultry.

THE PURINE CONTENT OF FOOD

High	Low
Yeast extracts	Tea
(such as Marmite)	Coffee
Bacon	Cereal
Liver	Cheese
Kidneys	Eggs
Sweetbreads	Milk

High
Sardines
Fish roes
Anchovies
Whitebait
Yeast, as in beer

KIDNEY FUNCTION

The other influential factor on the body's level of uric acid is the way in which the body gets rid of it. Some of the body's uric acid is excreted in sweat, and some of it by passing into the digestive system where it meets bacteria that are capable of breaking it down. But by far the majority of uric acid passes through the kidneys and is excreted in the urine. Damage to the kidneys can interfere with their ability to get rid of uric acid.

This is where alcohol comes in. The more alcohol you drink, the more lactic acid you will produce in your blood. Lactic acid, in turn, is known to affect the kidneys and to make them less efficient at eliminating uric acid.

It is not hard to see, then, that the more food you eat (so producing more uric acid) and the more alcohol you drink (so eliminating less uric acid), the more likely you are to develop gout. So it is hardly surprising that gout is associated with rich living.

There is, indeed, some justification for this. Publicans, hoteliers, brewery workers, all professions where over-indulgence in alcohol is something of an occupational hazard, as well as businessmen who have frequent business lunches, have a higher incidence of gout than those who follow more abstemious walks of life.

WEIGHT WATCHING

A lot of people with arthritis find that they put on weight, although they are eating only a normal amount of food and no more than they ate before they developed arthritis. This is usually because they have become significantly less mobile, with the result that their bodies do not get the chance to burn off surplus energy and the energy is consequently converted into fat.

No matter that the doctors don't agree about what you should eat for arthritis. One thing they do agree on is that to be overweight if you also have arthritis is a serious disadvantage.

Think about it and you will see that it makes sense. Why carry more weight on that arthritic joint than you have to? It is the weight-bearing joints that are most at risk from extra weight. These are found in the spine, legs and feet. Every extra pound you are carrying will only make your day that much more difficult.

Still doubtful? Well, try the following experiment. Weigh out a stone (14lb) of books on the bathroom scales. Then try lugging them up and down the stairs a few times. That should convince you!

Not only will being overweight make life more difficult for someone with arthritis, but it has also been found that people who are overweight are actually more likely to develop osteoarthritis. This is partly because of the extra load on the load-bearing joints but it is not only for that reason, since people who are overweight are also more likely to develop osteoarthritis in non-load-bearing joints, such as in their fingers and hands.

So lose those extra pounds – and keep them off. This is easier said than done. People who have a lot of time on their hands, or who feel unwell and depressed, often turn to food as a form of comfort or entertainment.

The only thing that can be said is that it is well worth losing weight for the sake of your joints if nothing else. Losing weight can actually slow down the rate of deterioration and may even help alleviate symptoms. You might not enjoy the process of doing it, but you'll be jolly glad you've done it once it's over.

Don't go on a crash diet, though. These seldom work, they're not good for you, and they are actually rather unpleasant to follow. Not only that: the weight is typically regained in a very short time. The answer is to lose weight sensibly and slowly.

If you need to lose weight, consult your doctor, who should be able to help you or may refer you to a dietitian who will show you how to reduce your calorie intake.

There are no miracle cures for being overweight. Basically, shedding pounds can mean only one thing – that's eating less and teaching yourself new eating habits, which become second nature. There are several tips that should help you do this.

☐ Only eat when you are hungry.

☐ When you feel hungry, drink a cup of tea or a glass of water. This will take the edge off your hunger by filling your stomach, though only with liquid.

☐ Set yourself a realistic target, say two or three pounds a week. Eat what you want, not what people expect you to eat.

☐ Insist on smaller portions than usual.

☐ Eat little and often rather than infrequent big meals.

☐ Do not skip meals. You'll just feel ravenously hungry and overeat at the next opportunity.

☐ Eat plenty of raw vegetables, salads, fruit and nuts. These are not only good for you, they also need a lot of chewing and take longer to eat.

☐ Eat slowly.

☐ Don't resort to comfort food.

☐ Use a smaller plate than usual.

☐ Join a slimming organisation to help keep you motivated and to provide encouragement.

DO NOT LOSE TOO MUCH WEIGHT

Dieting is not always a good idea if you suffer from certain conditions. In the case of rheumatoid arthritis, for example, the inflammation in the joints actually uses up a substantial part of the body's energy, which often causes weight loss. Losing too much weight in this way can be bad for you.

The aim is not to end up as a skinny, undernourished person with arthritis. That, after all, is no better than being a fat person with arthritis.

It is rather to provide your body with the best possible nourishment for optimum health.

RANGE OF HEALTHY WEIGHTS FOR WOMEN AND MEN

WOMEN		MEN	
Height	**Weight**	**Height**	**Weight**
4' 10"	92-119lb	5' 2"	112-126lb
4' 11"	94-122lb	5' 3"	115-144lb
5' 0"	96-125lb	5' 4"	118-148lb
5' 1"	99-128lb	5' 5"	121-152lb
5' 2"	102-131lb	5' 6"	124-154lb
5' 3"	105-134lb	5' 7"	128-161lb
5' 4"	108-138lb	5' 8"	132-166lb
5' 5"	111-142lb	5' 9"	136-170lb
5' 6"	114-146lb	5' 10"	140-174lb
5' 7"	118-150lb	5' 11"	144-179lb
5' 8"	122-154lb	6' 0"	148-184lb
5' 9"	126-158lb	6' 1"	152-189lb
5' 10"	130-163lb	6' 2"	156-194lb
5' 11"	134-168lb	6' 3"	160-199lb
6' 0"	138-174lb	6' 4"	164-204lb

6 Special Treatments That Work

When orthodox treatments fail, it is hardly surprising that so many sufferers try less conventional forms of treatment. What follows is a look at some of the most popular alternative, or complementary, approaches.

THERAPIES BASED ON THE BODY'S FLOW OF ENERGY

ACUPUNCTURE

This is based on the Latin words acus, meaning needle, and punctus, meaning to puncture or prick. It is an ancient Chinese therapy, which has been practised for some 3,500 years, in which patients are treated by sticking needles into their skin at particular points.

The acupuncture points lie along invisible energy channels, known as 'meridians', which are believed to be connected to the internal organs. The insertion of needles is thought to unblock the flow of energy through the meridians. Very fine stainless steel needles with tiny heads are used, which you can hardly feel when they are inserted.

Acupuncture was first used by British doctors in the early 19th century, primarily for the relief of pain and the treatment of fever. The first edition of *The Lancet* in 1823 carried a detailed report of the successful use of acupuncture in treating rheumatism.

Acupuncture will not restore permanently damaged tissues. It is used in arthritis not as a curative therapy but to relieve pain. This is achieved by diverting or changing painful messages that pass to the brain from damaged tissues, and perhaps by stimulating the body's endorphins and encephalins, which act as its own 'painkillers'.

Some acupuncturists also use moxibustion in conjunction with treatment with needles. Moxibustion is the local application of heat to regulate, tone and supplement the body's flow of energy. The most common method is for the acupuncturist to place moxa, the shredded leaves of the common mugwort, over the acupuncture point. The moxa is lit until it becomes too hot and then removed. The number of times this process is repeated depends on the nature and severity of the complaint. An acupuncture needle is then inserted as usual.

DOES IT WORK?

When acupuncture was first introduced into the West, it was derided by sceptics. Now, however, the evidence for its efficacy is overwhelming and it can no longer be denied. Its role in pain relief is incontrovertible and it has even been used as the only form of analgesia in major surgery. By comparison, pain relief in arthritis must be chicken feed!

Acupuncturists treat more patients with arthritis than any other complaint. Both osteoarthritis and rheumatoid arthritis have been found to respond well to acupuncture. They are best treated in their milder, transient forms, before they become chronic and lead to degenerative changes that cause both restricted movement and severe pain.

Acupuncture usually provides only temporary relief and its effect does not last forever, though breaking the pain cycle can, in rare cases, actually produce permanent relief. How effective it is depends largely on the progress of the underlying disease.

It is worth trying, though you should not hold out too much hope. Even partial or temporary relief from pain can give you a breathing space, which can in itself be valuable. And you never know: you might be one of the lucky ones, for whom it will have a dramatic and lasting effect.

In one study of painful, swollen osteoarthritic knees, acupuncture was compared with injections of hydrocortisone. The hydrocortisone was more successful in reducing swelling, but the acupuncture relieved pain for a longer period of time.

So if you are suffering from severe pain that is not relieved no matter what you try, ask your doctor to put you in touch with a qualified acupuncturist. It's worth a try.

ACUPRESSURE

Everyone uses some sort of acupressure or finger massage whenever they press their hands against their forehead to relieve a headache. Also known as shiatsu, acupressure is an ancient Japanese art, which follows much the same principles as acupuncture but uses finger pressure instead of needles.

The therapy uses the same energy channels, or meridians, as acupuncture, which respond to various degrees of pressure from the fingers and knuckles. This is believed to bring pain relief, to minimise fatigue, and to stimulate the body's own ability to heal itself.

DOES IT WORK?

There are many sufferers who can testify to the benefits of acupressure in pain relief.

It is also possible to relieve pain by applying a form of do-it-yourself acupressure (*see Chapter 3*).

REFLEXOLOGY

Foot reflexology is closely related to acupuncture and acupressure, in that it is based on the same principle that a life force flows through the body along energy channels or meridians. The difference, however, is that the terminal points of these meridians lie in the feet.

The origins of reflexology date back to China at least 5,000 years ago, and to ancient Egypt in around 2500 B.C. There is also evidence of its use in more recent times by American Indian tribes and primitive African tribes.

But the first real advance in foot reflexology can be attributed to Dr William Fitzgerald, who was an American ear, nose and throat specialist and surgeon working in the early part of this century. He discovered that he was able to limit the pain experienced by a patient by applying pressure to certain areas of the body. In time, he developed his theory of zone therapy and mapped out the pathways of the body into ten equal longitudinal zones – five on each side of a central line through the body – each one of which ended in the hands and feet. These are parts of the body with the least depth to them, which means the meridians are easier both to reach and to manipulate.

Reflexologists regard the feet as a 'mirror' of the body, with the left foot mirroring the left-hand side of the body, and the right foot mirroring the right-hand side. Massage alone is believed to trigger the body into healing itself.

Using the thumbs and fingers, the qualified therapist will restore the energy flow to its correct balance by massaging and stimulating various terminals in the feet, and will thus improve both the general circulation and the function of the specific glands and organs.

DOES IT WORK?

Some people have found reflexology to be of particular value in relieving the pain of arthritis. It is not always appropriate, however, for someone who has arthritis in the feet, though it may be possible to stimulate corresponding reflex points in the hands, provided the patient does not also have arthritis in the hands. Reflexology is also relaxing and eases stress.

But the important thing is to consult a qualified reflexologist. It is not, on the whole, a self-help measure, though once you have seen a therapist you may be able to help in the continuation of the therapy.

MANIPULATIVE THERAPIES

OSTEOPATHY

Osteopathy, based on the Greek words 'osteo', meaning bone, and 'pathos', meaning suffering, works on the theory that diseases can be treated by the manipulation of bones and, indirectly, of muscles, blood vessels and nerves.

It was started in the mid 1870s by an American doctor, Andrew Taylor Still, who had become disenchanted with orthodox medicines. He was fascinated by the idea of the body as a machine, and became convinced that many illnesses arise when part of the body's intricate structure goes out of alignment. It followed, he felt, that manipulation could restore the alignment and thus cure the illness.

Osteopathy did not come to Britain until the turn of this century. The British School of Osteopathy was set up in London in 1917 by Dr Martin Littlejohn, who was one of Dr Still's pupils. Osteopathy is now generally accepted as a respectable therapy and is one of the most widely used of all the complementary forms of medicine.

So talk to your doctor about the possibility of consulting an osteopath. He may well be able to recommend one.

The osteopath will take a general case history. He will want to know in particular how your symptoms first began and what makes them better or worse. He will also give you a full physical examination, and will observe how you stand, sit and lie down. He will assess the range and quality of your movements, as well as examining by touch the soft tissues, muscles and ligaments to assess whether they are in any way abnormally tense or stressed. An osteopath may also ask that a special osteopathic X-ray be taken, particularly if there has been any serious accident or major illness.

If the osteopath deems that your condition is suitable for treatment, he will devise a plan of action. This can include a number of approaches. He may use massage of soft tissues, which is relaxing and improves the circulation. In addition, the gentle, repetitive movement of joints increases their mobility.

Finally – and this is probably what most people associate with osteopathy – misaligned joints may be put back into their correct position by putting the joint rapidly through the normal range of movement. This gives rise to the characteristic clicking sounds.

As such, osteopathy is a corrective, rather than curative form of treatment. It can actually aggravate actively inflamed joints, but it can provide enormous relief in cases of neck and back pain caused by wear and tear on the spinal joints and discs.

DOES IT WORK?

In one survey of patients attending a rheumatism clinic in London, when they were asked which alternative forms of treatment they had tried and with what results, osteopathy was the only one that had struck them as being truly helpful.

There is no evidence that it can actually reverse degenerative changes but the sheer relief after a session can be quite fantastic. It is particularly effective in the short-term relief of back and neck pain.

It is very important, however, that treatment be given to the right person in the right way, otherwise it can be dangerous particularly when applied to the neck. It is therefore most important to find a reputable osteopath whose methods have been tried, tested and recommended.

Do not have any manipulative therapy if any of your joints are actively inflamed as it may aggravate these.

CHIROPRACTIC

The word chiropractic is based on the Greek words 'kheir', meaning hand, and 'practikos', meaning practical. It relies on the skilful use of the hands to correct disorders of the joints, muscles and in particular the spine.

In some ways, chiropractic is similar to osteopathy in that neither method uses drugs or surgery, and both are manipulative therapies. The main difference, however, is that chiropractors make greater use of X-rays and other conventional methods of diagnosis than osteopaths.

The chiropractor will take a medical history at the first consultation. He will then examine you physically, paying particular attention to any areas of pain, soreness and muscle spasm. He will also assess which joints are moving properly and which are not. He will probably ask for an X-ray to be taken, which may confirm signs of arthritis or bone disease.

Treatment, which will not usually begin until the second session, entails a series of manipulations of the joints. These will help restore normal movement to the joints, as well as relaxing the muscles that control them. The adjustment should not be painful.

Some patients will experience immediate relief from pain. Others may feel a dull ache, soreness or stiffness later that day or the following morning. Chronic complaints require more treatments than acute cases.

DOES IT WORK?

Chiropractic can be an effective form of relief from arthritis, particularly if it is begun in the early stages of disease. Always ask your doctor's advice before embarking on any manipulative therapy and be sure to go to a recommended therapist.

Do not have chiropractic if you are suffering from active inflammation of a joint, as it may aggravate the condition.

ALEXANDER TECHNIQUE

The Alexander Technique is designed both to treat and then to prevent a variety of disorders by an apparently simple system of postural changes that enable the body to work in a more natural, relaxed and efficient way. It is believed to promote harmony of both mind and body, and to be both effective and completely safe.

This therapy was first developed by an Australian actor, Frederick Matthias Alexander, who worked on himself for many years to treat the inexplicable loss of his voice on stage. He found that he could cure his problem by the relatively simple, not to say surprising, means of improving his posture. He had been pulling his head backwards and downwards and sucking in his breath whenever he wanted to speak. He succeeded in teaching himself to stop doing this and his voice returned to normal.

Alexander's discovery became the basis for a comprehensive technique of retraining the body's movements and positions. He began to teach his technique. In 1904, he came to London where he found himself in great demand, particularly by the acting profession, which soon recognised the advantages of his method.

He moved to America and his technique soon won international acclaim. At the age of 78, Alexander suffered a stroke. He was to astound his doctors by using his technique to regain the use of his body and all his faculties.

By this time, it was obvious that far more serious complaints could be treated by the Alexander Technique than just the occasional loss of an actor's voice. In 1973, the Dutch zoologist and ethnologist, Professor Nikolaas Tinbergen, winner of the Nobel Prize for Physiology and Medicine, said that "stress-related ailments could benefit from the Alexander Technique, including various forms of arthritis".

The technique is concerned with the proper use of the whole body. For most of us, that means changing the bad habits of a lifetime. This cannot be self-taught. It requires a qualified teacher to manipulate your body into a more natural position and to show you a new way of practising good posture. After a course of 30 or so lessons, you should have learned enough to be able to continue on your own.

DOES IT WORK?

If you watch any practitioner of the Alexander Technique, you will see that it does indeed teach someone all over again to sit, stand and walk with the natural ease of a child. Success has been claimed in treating many disorders, including both rheumatoid arthritis and osteoarthritis, as well as lower back pain and sciatica. Although doctors may not always suggest this therapy to their patients, they do not oppose it either.

ROLFING

Rolfing has some similarities to the Alexander Technique. It too is a form of 'structural processing', named after its originator, American biological chemist, Dr Ida Rolf who spent some 40 years formulating her technique of manipulation. She believed that many health problems are caused by bad posture, such as stooped shoulders and hunched backs. It is because someone is constantly trying to rectify this that they are drained of vitality and the normal working of their bodies is impaired – so making them vulnerable to illness.

To combat this, Dr Rolf formulated a complex manipulative system, which she termed 'structural reintegration'. By massaging the body's connective tissue and muscles, she aimed to restore the body to its correct alignment, so that all its physical structures were once again in a straight vertical line. She believed that only when the body was correctly aligned could the earth's field of gravity support the body's own energy field, and only then could true physical and psychological well-being be achieved.

DOES IT WORK?

Rolfing is aimed at anyone who feels that their body structure is in any way out of alignment and would welcome the opportunity to correct this. It is generally considered to be rather a way of learning about the body than a specific treatment for any particular disorder.

A standard Rolfing course usually consists of ten one-hour sessions spread over several weeks. As such, it is a fairly expensive, though interesting, way of doing this.

NATURAL CURES

HOMOEOPATHY

The origins of homoeopathy go back as far as 1810, when a German physician called Samuel Hahnemann put forward a new system of medicine as an alternative to the orthodox medicine of the day. Orthodox medicine then included practices such as bloodletting and purging, which Hahnemann believed to be too harsh and often to weaken patients more than their illnesses did.

Hahnemann believed that a person's symptoms are the result of the body trying to resist the attack. "Far from seeking a way to suppress symptoms," he wrote, "it may be desirable to take some form of treatment calculated to help the resistance."

His theory of how this could be done was inspired by the discovery that a herbal remedy for malaria, cinchona tree bark, actually produced symptoms of the disease, such as fever and headache, when it was taken by a healthy person. Hahnemann's ideas were, in effect, a version of an ancient principle first formulated by the Greek physician Hippocrates in the fifth century B.C., 'like cures like'.

The orthodox doctor would prescribe a drug that lowers the temperature for a patient with a fever. The homoeopath, on the other hand, would prescribe one to raise the temperature, because fever is the body's natural way of fighting off the disease.

Hahnemann called his system homoeopathy, from the Greek words 'homoios', meaning like, and 'pathos', meaning suffering. He believed that small doses of homoeopathic medicine would be safer than big ones, and actually went further than that and argued that the more dilute the dose the greater its effectiveness – a paradox that still puzzles many conventional doctors to the point of disbelief.

He spent many years experimenting both on himself and on his family and friends, using a wide range of natural substances in very dilute forms. His approach was a 'holistic' one, in that it aimed to treat the whole person – mental, emotional, spiritual and physical – and not just the symptoms or the disease.

The homoeopath will take a medical history and ask you many questions, some of which like "Are you frightened of thunderstorms?" and "Do you prefer hot or cold weather?" may seem a little odd. This is because he is trying to assess certain things about you as a whole person, such as your personality, your manner and appearance, your mood and state of mind, your beliefs, hopes and fears.

Homoeopathy, remember, aims to treat the whole person, not just the disease. So it is this detailed assessment, just as much as your symptoms, that will help the homoeopath decide on a suitable course of treatment.

In most cases, homoeopaths prescribe only a single dose of one remedy and wait to see what its effects are before offering any further treatment. Any changes are seen as evidence that the remedy is working and is boosting the body's healing process.

But for long-term, chronic conditions such as arthritis, treatment has to be monitored over a long period of time and may have to be changed if improvement ceases or any new symptoms develop.

DOES IT WORK?

There are many homoeopaths who prescribe for arthritis and who claim that their remedies are still more effective than conventional treatments. The world-famous heart surgeon Christian Barnard, himself a long-time sufferer from rheumatoid arthritis, considers homoeopathy to be interesting as an effective remedy for arthritis, though he says that "so far the merits are not proven".

Clinical trials on homoeopathy have yielded varying results. Some have claimed success, while others have shown no significant difference between one homoeopathic remedy for arthritis and a placebo (a medicine with no curative effect).

The conclusions are not certain one way or the other. One thing, however, is certain: homoeopathy is unlikely to do you any harm. So if you're tempted to try it, do.

But make sure you consult a properly qualified homoeopath. Many qualified homoeopaths are not medically qualified. Some, however, are also qualified medical doctors, and a lot of people would say that you are better off choosing one of these. In this way, you will get the best of both disciplines.

BACH REMEDIES

Bach remedies are a series of 38 preparations made from wild plants and flowers, named after their originator, who was an English physician practising in the early 20th century, called Dr Edward Bach. Dr Bach was a medical doctor and bacteriologist in London in 1915, who also practised homoeopathy and was a great believer in the power of natural cures.

He was himself seriously ill in 1917, when he discovered that he was able to judge the healing properties of different plants by some kind of innate intuition. In 1930, he gave up his successful Harley Street practice and settled in Wales, where he continued in his search for healing plants.

Dr Bach would collect the flowers in the early morning, when they were still covered in dew. He would choose only the truly perfect specimens and would distil their essence either by boiling them gently in pure water, or by steeping them in pure cold water for three hours in full sunlight. In this way, he was able to bottle his remedies, and the same production methods are still used today.

Bach remedies are intended to treat the whole person and not just the symptoms of disease. They are chosen according to psychological and emotional characteristics and work on the principle that every disorder comes about because of an inner imbalance. Dr Bach believed that, for every disorder, nature has provided a remedy in the form of healing plants, spring water, fresh air and sunlight.

Bach remedies come in a concentrated form, preserved in alcohol. They can be taken either in a little water or dropped straight onto the tongue.

DO THEY WORK?

Bach remedies have a pleasing simplicity. They are said to be safe for babies and children, and even for animals.

If you are tempted by this, you can either buy them yourself from many health food shops and chemists, or you can find a Bach therapist, many of whom also practise homoeopathy, herbalism or naturopathy.

Many people will confirm the effectiveness of Bach remedies, though science can find no explanation for their claims. They cannot do you any harm, anyway, so may be worth trying.

HERBALISM

Herbalism is not new. Until the 18th century, it was, in fact, the most common form of medical treatment in the West and can be viewed as the precursor of modern pharmacology. Even today, the World Health Organisation estimates that it is three or four times more commonly practised world-wide than conventional medicine.

Some of the most famous names in modern medicine started out as herbalists. Thomas Beecham, for example, founder of the multi-national pharmaceutical conglomerate, began his career as a herbalist, as did John Boot, whose son, Jesse, founded Britain's renowned chain of chemist's shops.

The use of herbs for healing purposes has gained enormous support, and herbal medicine is once again popular. There is an ever-increasing number of herbalists who treat patients, and they claim their medicines can help most people suffering from most kinds of illness, including chronic conditions such as arthritis.

At the initial consultation, the herbalist will take a medical history, and will ask questions about the patient's life-style as well as about his present state of health. He will give general advice on improving his general health, and will prescribe a chosen course of treatment. This can take several forms, including a herbal tincture, a lotion, a cream or an ointment.

DOES IT WORK?

Herbal medicines generally work more slowly than conventional medicines, especially with long-standing disorders. But the idea is that, as the herbs begin to enhance the body's natural healing powers, so the patient will soon start to feel better in himself.

The herbal remedies used in arthritis are generally more likely to relieve pain than to cure – usually in the form of lotions, creams and baths – and even these provoke little more than puzzled disbelief in many sceptics. But a lot of people with arthritis swear by them and, since pain relief is half the battle, they may be worth trying.

AROMATHERAPY

Aromatherapy is the art of using the healing properties of essential oils derived from plants. Essential oils can be used in a variety of ways, though in Britain they are used mostly for massage treatments. Massage is believed to be a particularly valuable treatment for the relief of stress and pain around the joints. It also improves mobility in the stiffness of a joint.

Essential oils can also be inhaled, added to baths – or, if the patient finds it difficult to get into the bath, used in foot and hand baths – and used for compresses. Baths and compresses have been found to be effective pain relievers by many people who suffer from arthritis.

DOES IT WORK?

Judging by the number of devotees, aromatherapy can be most helpful. Conventional doctors are becoming increasingly aware of the benefits of aromatherapy, to such an extent that many hospitals now use it as part of their regime.

HYPNOTHERAPY

Hypnotherapy is based on the Greek word 'hypnos', meaning sleep. And it is through a state of consciousness somewhere between wakefulness and sleep that hypnotherapists try to improve a person's state of health.

Unfortunately, hypnosis still holds some fear for many people, whether as something rather sinister and menacing, or as a tool of stage ridicule. But hypnosis has a long history of treating pain and is, increasingly, becoming a respected form of therapy.

If, for example, your arthritis is thought to be linked with excessive stress or anxiety, hypnotherapy could be used to suspend your conscious mind and to allow the deeper levels of the mind to become open to the powers of suggestion. In this way, hypnotherapy can be used to put suggestions in the unconscious mind. It cannot heal or cure, but it can provoke certain reactions that may, ultimately, bring about relief of the condition.

Hypnotherapy has been used as a painkiller since the mid-19th century, when surgeons performed many operations using hypnosis as the only anaesthetic. The power of hypnosis over pain is therefore unquestionable, and it is in this capacity that it is of greatest use in the treatment of arthritis.

DOES IT WORK?

It can only work if you trust your therapist totally and you feel quite calm and relaxed. If you have any serious reservations about the treatment, it probably won't work. Some people are more susceptible to hypnosis than others.

But many people with arthritis have found their pain to be reduced and their mobility improved following hypnotherapy. It is becoming increasingly accepted by the medical profession, so your doctor may be able to recommend a hypnotherapist, if not perform the therapy himself – something that more and more doctors are now trained to do.

7 What Can The Doctors Do To Help You?

Articles written for doctors about how they should treat people with arthritis usually start with the same thing – not with drugs, surgery or even physiotherapy – but with education. Helping people understand what is wrong with them, so that they can play a constructive role in managing it, is an important component in modern medicine. It is especially important with a condition like arthritis which, while not putting you in hospital, is likely to remain with you off and on for the rest of your life.

It cannot be emphasised enough that, although there is as yet no cure for arthritis, the diagnosis does not have to be a message of doom. These days there is a lot that doctors, and above all, the arthritis sufferer him or herself, can do to minimise the physical symptoms and restrictions involved. There are four good reasons to be optimistic if you learn you have arthritis:

1. Only a small percentage of sufferers are severely incapacitated by the disease.
2. Positive attitudes make illness more tolerable.
3. Medical treatments – drugs, injections, surgery and artificial joints – are getting better every year.
4. Research is moving so fast that a cure for some forms of arthritis may not be far away.

In many ways it pays to be a demanding patient. This is not the same as being a hypochondriac. It implies being prepared to take expert advice to modify your life-style and to try treatment and medication that may improve things. Doctors and therapists welcome the active involvement of patients in their care. Rheumatologist Ian Haslock, writing recently in the medical journal *Doctor* said: "Patients have higher expectations nowadays. In the past they were willing to be fobbed off with the advice 'there's nothing can be done for arthritis', and would accept progressive disability as an inevitable consequence of their disease. They are now more knowledgeable and generally less tolerant of symptoms." We will start by looking at the treatment options as they apply to all the main forms of the disease and then go on to consider those that are specific to a particular condition.

TREATMENT OR CURE?

It may be useful to draw a distinction between these two words because at some stage you will probably hear arthritis described as 'incurable'. The term has gloomy associations and is enough to make anyone with a disease give up completely, a temptation which you should resist. However, from the point of view of the doctors and medical researchers the distinction is important. Their goal is to understand the processes that attack the joints so that they can reverse the damage, or prevent any further damage occurring. At the moment all they can do is treat the symptoms of the disease, limit damage to the joints sometimes and hope that the attack will limit itself (what doctors call remission).

THE GOALS OF TREATMENT

There is broad agreement that in arthritis these are:
- the relief of pain and discomfort;
- maintaining maximum use of the affected joints;
- correcting the disease process when possible.

To these we add, and make no apology for going on about it:

- keeping up the patient's spirits. In fact this objective probably comes before all the other three and certainly contributes to the success of the first two.

KINDS OF TREATMENT

The medical experts, which include your doctor, possibly a hospital specialist, together with the occupational therapist and physiotherapist who are part of the team, will advise on all aspects of treatment, including diet, exercise and modifications to your home. Kinds of treatment come under five headings:

1. Drugs and injections.
2. Exercise, rest, manipulation, physiotherapy.
3. Local heat: lamps, rubs, electrical stimulation.
4. Life-style adjustments: diet, useful gadgets.
5. Surgery.

The mainstay of medical treatment for arthritis (with the possible exception of gout, for which there is a drug that controls the disease process itself) is painkilling and/or anti-inflammatory drugs. There are so many it would be pointless and confusing to tell you about each individual drug, but we will describe the main groups, how they work and what the side-effects could be, so that you will be able to understand the choices your doctor offers you.

Drugs. Many people are very reluctant to take drugs, even the humble, common-or-garden aspirin, which happens to be an invaluable aid in the treatment of mild arthritis. The well-known British 'stiff upper lip' leads us to pride ourselves on concealing our feelings and human frailty and to see virtue in the stalwart endurance of discomfort: cold bedrooms, bad food or physical pain.

It is not weak, let alone wicked to take pills
for arthritis; it's good medicine and
good common sense!

That said, you should not treat serious and continuous joint pain with vast quantities of aspirin or any other painkiller bought over the counter at your local chemist. Arthritis is a serious enough condition to require medical supervision. There is much you can do at home to help yourself, but always be guided by your doctor and the medical experts in what you do, and especially in what you take.

Painkilling (analgesic) drugs. Many of the commonest drugs for arthritis are both painkilling and anti-inflammatory. For example, *aspirin* – a drug originally derived from willow bark, and known to primitive tribes – both dulls pain and reduces fever and inflammation, which is why it is a good treatment for the common cold or toothache. However, as many of us know, aspirin and a large group of painkilling drugs called nonsteroidal anti-inflammatory drugs (NSAIDs for short) can irritate the stomach and digestive tract. So if your arthritis is the non-inflammatory kind – as most osteoarthritis is – the doctor will start by recommending simple painkillers that don't risk this side-effect.

The best-known trouble-free painkiller is *paracetamol*. Less well-known and slightly stronger – hence available on prescription only – is *dextropropoxyphene* which is combined with paracetamol in two common painkillers, *Distalgesic* and *Co-proxamol*, and a number of compounds containing codeine. Paracetamol has no side-effects, although it is unsuitable for anyone whose liver has been damaged, by hepatitis for example. Combined with paracetamol, *codeine* provides even better pain control, though it can cause constipation. Long-acting *dihydroceine (DHC Continus)* is particularly successful as a night-time painkiller. Both codeine and dextropropoxyphene can occasionally cause dizziness, drowsiness and slight nausea. *Mefenamic acid (Ponstan)* is another simple painkiller with minimal side-effects. In common with paracetamol, all these drugs can be dangerous if taken in overdose.

Choosing a painkiller. Pain relief is subjective and therefore highly personal. If one painkiller doesn't seem to be doing the job, don't be afraid to ask your doctor to prescribe you another.

Localised pain relief. Swallowing pills is not the only way that the medical team can help you control pain. There are several localised pain relief techniques often recommended by the physiotherapy department which are particularly useful for resistant pain. In principle they are sophisticated ways of delivering heat to the inside of the joint. They include *short-wave diathermy* in which short-wave electromagnetic energy is beamed, or nowadays probably pulsed through the joint; nothing touches you and you feel nothing. Very high-frequency sound waves called *ultrasound* can also be used to generate heat inside the joint; the joint is put next to the machine, and again you feel nothing. Both these treatments are done in the clinic. The third, *transcutaneous electrical nerve stimulation*, or TENS, in which a pulse of low-frequency electrical current, generated by a little battery, is transmitted to the nerve by means of small terminals taped to the skin, can also be supplied as portable equipment for you to use at home. If you have ever had the electric output of your heart measured, it looks a little like this. All you will feel is a slight tingling like pins and needles.

Anti-inflammatory drugs. Drugs prescribed for rheumatoid arthritis, or any form of arthritis that includes inflammation, have to perform three functions:

1) control pain;
2) reduce stiffness and swelling;
3) reduce inflammation and the damage this causes to the tissues of the joint.

Your doctor will probably prescribe either a form of aspirin (*Disprin* or *Nu-Seals Aspirin*), or possibly one of the *NSAIDs* (non-steroid anti-inflammatory drugs), which have fewer side-effects than aspirin when, as is necessary for an anti-inflammatory effect, they are taken in high doses. Another very successful drug is *omeprazole (Losec)*.

Corticosteroids are very effective anti-inflammatory drugs. Because of their side-effects, they are used only sporadically to cover acute attacks and to top up other drugs. Used with NSAIDs, they are more likely to produce gastrointestinal complications such as ulcers.

There are more than 25 tried and tested anti-inflammatory drugs for a doctor to choose from. Their abundance reflects both their important role in treating widespread diseases and the fact that no one drug is manifestly superior to another. 'Old favourites' include *ibuprofen (Brufen), indomethacin (Indocid),* and *naproxen (Naprosyn).* All NSAIDs can cause stomach irritation or even ulceration. Some also cause skin rashes or fluid retention (when your ankles get puffy) and this can have a bad effect on heart function and your breathing. However, not everyone suffers from these side-effects, and the manufacturers have tried to counteract the most common by devising special preparations of drugs. Some are coated to delay absorption in the stomach, or are available as suppositories which are absorbed via the rectum, or as gels to be applied externally, directly to the joint, though all these are not equally effective against inflammation, or as acceptable to the patient.

If indigestion or stomach irritation troubles you, the doctor may suggest an extra pill that will reduce the amount of acid produced in your stomach, a beta-blocker like *cimetidine (Tagamet)* or *ranitidine (Zantac),* or *Cytotec* which contains the drug *misoprostol.* As with straightforward painkillers, you need to find the anti-inflammatory drug that's best for you. If you get side-effects from one ask your doctor for a different prescription.

SIDE-EFFECTS

A full list of the possible side-effects of NSAIDs could easily encourage alarm. Remember that drug manufacturers are required by law to list all the side-effects that have ever been noted in trials of their drugs, even when these were extremely rare or affected very few people, or only those who were suffering some other major health problem. A lot of side-effects show up only if doctors do special tests; you don't actually feel any symptoms. The safest thing is tell your doctor if you notice anything new or unpleasant when taking a drug and let her be the judge of whether the drug could be responsible. She will take tests to keep tabs on how your body is functioning and knows what to look for.

STEROID INJECTIONS

Occasionally the doctor may try injecting an anti-inflammatory drug – a corticosteroid like *methylprednisolone* – into an actively inflamed joint. This is helpful for the knees, shoulders and thumbs, though only if a few joints are affected. Delivering drugs direct into the affected area is also helpful for patients who do not tolerate NSAIDs well and can provide relief for as long as four months. Side-effects are rare, but there is some evidence that corticosteroids can speed up degeneration of the joint so they are not usually given for long periods; they also interact with NSAIDs and are therefore not usually given together.

DRUGS INTERACT

The effect of one drug upon another is a constant problem for doctors especially when treating elderly patients who may be taking several different pills for different medical conditions. Make sure they know about any pills you take for any other condition or for whatever reason.

OTHER INJECTIONS

An injection may also be used to take fluid out of a painfully swollen joint. If it is necessary to do this frequently, other drugs such as *osmic acid* or *yttrium* may be introduced into the joint to reduce inflammation at the same time. Failing this, surgery to remove the inflamed membrane may eventually be considered (*see section on surgery*).

REMINDER: KEEP TAKING THE TABLETS!

Pain with arthritis tends to come and go. It may be worse at some times of day, after some activities and in certain weather. You may therefore have a problem remembering to take your pills regularly. If you have difficulty you could ask your doctor to prescribe one of the new long-acting pain-killers.
Studies show that more than two thirds of people taking pills four times a day forget to take them, whereas less than a third have problems if it's only once a day.

ANTI-RHEUMATOID DRUGS

These drugs come under the heading of those that affect the actual process of the disease as well as treating symptoms. The doctors refer to them as second-line drugs. Exactly how some of these drugs work is uncertain and, as with painkillers and anti-inflammatory drugs, not all patients show progress, or suffer the same side-effects. The same process of trial and error is necessary in establishing what works best for you, and, in the case of anti-rheumatoid drugs, this will take some time because they only start to affect the disease after weeks or even months.

In the past doctors often delayed the use of second-line drugs for rheumatoid arthritis until the disease was quite advanced and damage to the joint had become structural. Today the trend is for more so-called aggressive treatment, starting these drugs early after diagnosis, before any damage to the joints shows up on X-ray, and continuing as long as they are preventing joint erosion and the side-effects are not serious. Side-effects are quite common with anti-rheumatoid drugs and doctors may switch your medication several times until the optimum combination of drugs for each individual patient is achieved. Your doctor may be happy to prescribe some of these drugs, or, because of the necessity of keeping a constant check on the effect they have on important body processes, she may prefer to refer you to a consultant rheumatologist at the nearest hospital.

The principal anti-rheumatoid drugs are:

Gold. This was first tried for the treatment of rheumatoid arthritis in the 1920s following its use in combating tuberculosis. It can be given by injection into a muscle – weekly to begin with; less frequently when the drug begins to work – or, nowadays by mouth. Oral gold can cause diarrhoea, but other side-effects are unlikely.

Auranofin (Ridaura). There is a risk of skin rashes and you will have to have blood tests to check that it doesn't reduce the number of white cells you produce (important disease-fighting substances), and urine tests to check that your kidneys are functioning normally.

Sulphasalazine (Salazopyrin). This drug has been around for more than 50 years but has recently come into common use again. It is given as pills, by mouth, in gradually increasing doses. Occasionally patients feel a little sick while adjusting to the drug but this usually doesn't persist. Recently the manufacturers have improved the acceptability of this drug by coating it to delay absorption in the stomach.

D-penicillamine (Distamine or Pendramine). This antibiotic drug, distantly related to penicillin, was found to have an anti-rheumatoid effect 30 years ago. It can be used quite safely even by people who are allergic to penicillin. Patients start with quite a low dose which is gradually increased over a period of weeks. Although chemically quite different from gold, the drug works in a similar way, is equally successful, but requires the same kind of precautions. Occasionally people notice a metallic taste in the mouth when first taking it.

CHLOROQUINE (AVLOCLOR OR NIVAQUINE) AND HYDROXYCHLOROQUINE (PLAQUENIL)

These drugs were found to have a good effect on a rare form of arthritis called systemic lupus erythematosus that is accompanied by a skin rash, and then tried successfully with rheumatoid arthritis. They are slightly less effective than the first three drugs on the list, and high doses given over a long period may affect the eyes, so it is customary to have regular eye check-ups if you take them.

The five anti-rheumatic drugs mentioned were found to be effective in the treatment of rheumatoid arthritis by fortunate accident – serendipity, which plays a surprisingly important role in the development of drug treatments even today. Doctors admit that, although there are theories as to how they work, they are still not proven. It's a question of trial and error, seeing how things work in practice and being prepared to juggle treatment around to suit the individual patient. This is not the way doctors prefer to work. They are happier when they know exactly what a drug does and how this relates to the disease process. Only when this is achieved is there any hope of a genuine cure, or, better still, preventive treatment.

VARYING DOSAGE

Sometimes inflammation of the joints will flare up again if, because of side-effects, treatment with D-penicillamine, or intramuscular gold is stopped abruptly. For this reason the amount you take is always increased and decreased gradually.

IMMUNOSUPPRESSIVE DRUGS

There is a fifth group of drugs used to treat rheumatoid arthritis that in practice is no better or worse than the compounds that have been in use over many years, but which operate by modifying what doctors currently believe is the cause of the disease. These are the immunosuppressive drugs.

In the very simplest terms, the body has natural defence mechanisms usually employed to fight invading viruses or bacteria, or any foreign body – a splinter in your finger, or a blood transfusion with blood that doesn't match your own. If you have ever had a splinter go 'septic' you will know that part of this mechanism produces inflammation and swelling, and will eventually push out the intrusive splinter. This mechanism is known as the auto-immune mechanism because the body recognises itself and normally protects itself (auto) from attack and only rejects foreign bodies. In the case of rheumatoid arthritis, the system fails to recognise its own tissue and turns these defence mechanisms against some part of our own bodies, producing inflammation, swelling and eventually, the destruction of the part attacked: in this case the membrane that lines the joint – the synovium.

Immunosuppressive drugs do what their name says: they suppress this natural response in the body and thereby reduce inflammation and the damage that follows. Several of these drugs are now used in the treatment of rheumatoid arthritis: *methotrexate (Maxtrex), azathioprine (Imuran), cyclophosphamide (Endoxana)* and *chlorambucil (Leukeran)*. Used alone, or in combination with other anti-arthritic drugs, they often produce a dramatic improvement in symptoms, including complete remission for several years. However they are potent drugs which affect the whole auto-immune system, not just that concerned with inflammation of the joints. They are therefore almost always given under the close supervision of a specialist rheumatology department which monitors the function of important organs in the body that can be damaged by prolonged use of these drugs.

Immunosuppressant drugs effectively turn off the body's defence mechanisms. This leaves you exposed to all sorts of infections against which they might otherwise defend you. Nevertheless, our understanding of the complex processes at work in the immune system is constantly advancing and medical experts are now certain that immunotherapy will play a vital role in the future management of rheumatoid arthritis. Drugs are being developed that target the particular parts of the immune system involved in causing inflammation of the synovium. With these drugs, doctors are able to immobilise this process alone, rather than affecting the entire defence system (see *The Future* at the end of this chapter).

DRUGS TO TREAT GOUT

If you suffer an acute attack of gout the pain is pretty bad and the doctor will almost certainly prescribe a painkiller to start with. Aspirin is not recommended, and it may even precipitate an attack. The non-steroidals are useful. The NSAID *azapropazone (Rheumox)* can be used because it combines anti-inflammatory effects with a reduction in the production of uric acid – the chemical in the blood that breaks down to produce crystals inside the joints in gout. *Indomethacin (Indocid)* and *naproxen (Naprosyn)*, or any other non-steroidal, are also sometimes prescribed. They need to be used only for short periods, until preventive treatment begins to work, and therefore side-effects are unlikely. Occasionally people with a tendency to be allergic get a touch of indigestion, a rash, headache or dizziness or even asthma on NSAIDs. Anyone who has had stomach acid disorders, especially a peptic ulcer, must always remember to take painkilling tablets on a full stomach.

One long established treatment for acute gout is *colchicine* (obtained from the meadow saffron, or autumn crocus). Tablets are taken every two hours until the pain is relieved. The only side-effect is the risk of diarrhoea. Very occasionally, if the pain persists, your doctor may prescribe a *corticosteroid* to reduce the inflammation early in the attack. Acute gout is treated with non-steroidals, so don't start them within three weeks of acute gout or it will return.

These drugs treat the symptoms of gout as they do in other forms of arthritis. However, it is also possible to prevent attacks by lowering the levels of uric acid present in the blood. To start with your doctor will give you a list of the foods and drinks that encourage the production of uric acid so that you can avoid them. Liver, sweetbreads, kidneys and protein-rich meat, for example, should all be taken in moderation. This accords with modern ideas of healthy eating in any case. Following this diet may encourage you to lose a few pounds, which in addition to reducing the amount of uric acid in your blood stream, will, without doubt also lighten the load on your joints.

YOUR WEIGHT

Being overweight does not actually cause any form of arthritis, but it can certainly aggravate the symptoms, and the wear and tear on the joints in the case of osteoarthritis. If you are overweight your doctor will almost certainly recommend a reducing diet as part of your treatment programme. You put this into practice at home, but it is nevertheless an important part of your medical treatment (*see Chapter 5*).

In the past, modifying your diet was the only way to cut down uric acid levels in the blood. However, it is now known that gout is not necessarily the result of an over-indulgent life-style. Some people make excess uric acid without eating too much of those naughty foods; doctors can prescribe drugs that lower uric acid levels in the blood more efficiently than diet alone and prevent the crystals being deposited in the joints and other parts of the body where they cause pain, inflammation and ultimately damage.

MEDICINE ON THE MENU FOR THE REST OF YOUR LIFE

Preventive treatments for gout, like those for asthma and diabetes, will have to be taken every day without fail for the rest of your life, even in the absence of warning signs, so you have to be organised and disciplined to keep to the programme. The drug manufacturers do what they can to make things easy – the once-a-day treatment is the goal – but you yourself must ensure that you take your medication regularly, without fail.

The best-known preventive drug for gout is *allopurinol (Caplenal, Hamarin* and *Zyloric)*; this drug reduces the amount of uric acid you produce. There are two other drugs called *probenecid (Benemid)* and *sulphinpyrazone (Anturan)* which reduce the level of uric acid circulating in the blood by flushing it out through the kidneys. Both types are very safe and may be used for years with few side-effects. The only common side-effect is a skin rash that disappears when you stop taking the tablets. Just occasionally an acute attack of gout may occur when you start preventive treatment, in which case you will need to continue with the NSAID or colchicine you have been prescribed for pain relief for a little longer.

TAKING THE WATERS

Gout sufferers need to get into the habit of drinking plenty of water. This helps flush the uric acid in your system out through the kidneys.

TREATMENTS OTHER THAN DRUGS

The quantity of different drugs used to treat arthritis is partly due to the fact that, with the possible exception of gout, no one treatment is one hundred per cent satisfactory. When an illness cannot be cured or prevented, a whole armoury of therapeutic procedures has to be used to achieve the best results for the individual patient. Medical advances in the treatment of symptoms, and in the substitution of damaged parts have, in the case of arthritis, progressed ahead of prevention.

GETTING THE MEDICAL MIX RIGHT

When your doctor first diagnoses arthritis she cannot prescribe a single pill to put things right so that you can continue otherwise exactly as before. A whole range of things: patterns of posture, exercise and rest, changes of diet and life-style and even the organisation of your home, suddenly become the concern of the medical team, some of which they will carry out, others which you will organise with their guidance.

WHAT SURGERY CAN DO FOR YOU

Before we consider what the orthopaedic surgeon can do in terms of joint replacement, we outline briefly some operations carried out on arthritic joints which are less radical than total replacement.

Removal of the damaged membrane (synovectomy). This is not a common operation but is sometimes tried when someone with rheumatoid arthritis has not responded to anti-inflammatory or anti-rheumatic drugs, and when the membrane (synovium) has become so bulky and inflamed that it causes mechanical problems inside the joint, and threatens to damage the tendons and ligaments that contain it. The operation gives relief from inflammation for some years and may be useful in increasing the range of movement in an infected joint. It is only possible where the surgeon can gain easy access: for example, the knee, ankle, elbow or wrist. The surgery needs to be undertaken before the disease has reached the stage of eating away at the bone of the joint. Surgery cannot, of course, halt the progress of the arthritis elsewhere.

Removal of damaged tissue from the joint (debridement). Orthopaedic surgeons are sometimes reluctant to perform a hip or joint replacement in younger arthritis sufferers because the artificial joint may not last the patient's lifetime. This alternative minor surgical procedure has become more popular with the development of a slender fibre-optic probe called an arthroscope that can be inserted into a joint with minimal damage to the surrounding healthy tissue. The arthroscope can be used simply to investigate the state of a damaged joint: the 'scope' part of the name implies it is for looking; or it can be used, rather like a medical Hoover, to clear away damaged cartilage and the out-growths of bone produced by exposed bone in osteoarthritis. The surface of the remaining cartilage is usually roughened up to encourage new cartilage to form. This procedure causes minimal damage to the tissue around the affected joint – just a small hole in the skin where the fibre-optic cable has been inserted, and can be done under local anaesthetic. Debridement can delay the need for joint replacement for some years and is therefore especially useful for relatively young patients with osteoarthritis.

Bone shortening, straightening, realignment (osteotomy). Osteoarthritis of the hip or knee can be aggravated by one leg being a little longer than the other or by the bones of the joint becoming in some way misaligned. In these cases correcting the deficiency can slow down the progress of the disease and alleviate the discomfort in the joint. It is most successful in the knee or foot joints of younger, overweight patients, and may last up to 10 years, delaying the need for an artificial replacement. It may even stimulate the joint to heal. It does not, of course, remove the need to lose weight.

Bone fusion (arthrodesis). This is very much a last resort and only used when for some reason joint replacement is not a viable option and there is quite severe deformity in a joint. It can be quite successful between damaged vertebrae in the neck because the movement lost by the operation is not so great there to begin with, and it is also occasionally used for the wrist or ankle. It may be suitable if you are young and otherwise active but have a single damaged joint, and the likelihood of heavy wear makes an artificial joint unsuitable. In arthrodesis the joint is fixed permanently either by nailing or wiring the two parts together or by grafting in an extra piece of bone. Although movement in the joint is restricted still further, it ceases to be painful.

Splinting. Splinting, or other ways of keeping people immobile, used to be much more popular in the treatment of arthritis than today. It was used in cases of ankylosing spondylitis, as were corsets and braces, and only rarely did any good. It sometimes made things worse. The one occasion when splinting is still considered valuable today is when a young person, whose bones are still growing, develops arthritis. Occasionally splints are recommended in order that a child's joints will not become deformed by the disease. They usually only have to be worn at rest to ensure that a child's knees or wrists are in a good position when the child is in bed. This is because there is always the risk that when the child feels unwell and in pain, he may

105

curl up and his joints stiffen into a bad position. Sometimes in extreme circumstances, tendons may need lengthening surgically, or if a knee or foot grows seriously out of line, osteotomy may be recommended to correct the position of the bones.

CHILDREN WITH ARTHRITIS

Sadly, some 15,000 children a year suffer from a juvenile form of arthritis. Medical treatment for children follows what we have already outlined; pain control, reduction of inflammation and the right mix of exercise and rest. However, the use of corticosteroids to decrease inflammation can cause growth problems in young children and sometimes there is the need for additional medication to counteract this effect. Children's eyes also require special attention when they have rheumatoid arthritis; very rarely it may be necessary to operate upon them.

If your child develops arthritis it is obviously very worrying. Reassure yourself with the fact that most of them recover completely after months or a little more than a year, so the most important thing while the arthritis lasts is to avoid any permanent damage to their joints and general health or to their social and educational development. The Arthritis and Rheumatism Council has helpful booklets and a network of supportive fellow sufferers to help the parents of children with arthritis as well as for adult arthritis sufferers. You will find their address at the end of this book.

REPLACEMENT SURGERY

In many ways this is the glamorous side of arthritis: the Wonder of Modern Medicine story. However, although treatment has been revolutionised by the development of artificial spare parts (known as prostheses) most doctors look forward fervently to the day when they can treat arthritis by means of prevention and cure, rather than with open surgery.

That said, nearly every one of us has seen some newly vigorous person whose life has been transformed by a new hip or knee joint. For many years it is likely to be the treatment of choice for middle-aged people with persistent pain and loss of movement caused by osteoarthritis of these joints.

Replacement surgery is principally for osteoarthritis sufferers. It is occasionally used in cases of rheumatoid arthritis when the joint has become seriously deformed or intractably painful, but in inflammatory arthritis the preferred treatment is to avoid bone loss by controlling the inflammation with drugs or injections.

The ideal patient for a hip or knee replacement is not a young person because artificial joints are not designed to withstand heavy use over long periods. Success in joint replacement is measured by its still being in place 10 years later. Longer than 15 years and it is possible the joint may need to be replaced in a second operation. However, although not a stripling, you should be sufficiently active and in good general health to benefit from the increased mobility that comes with a replacement and to be able to undertake the quite strenuous rehabilitation programme that follows the operation. Hip replacements have been performed the longest; they are marginally easier to do. However, with modern techniques and materials, knee replacements are becoming more common and at least as successful. You will also now occasionally meet someone who has had a shoulder or elbow replacement or even artificial hand joints.

In a total joint replacement (arthroplasty) the joint is opened up under general anaesthetic, the damaged surface of the joint is completely cut out and new artificial components made from metal (usually stainless steel), together with metal-backed high density polyethylene, are put in their place. These materials are used because they cause very little friction and therefore stand up well to wear and tear in use. The new components are usually held in place with a special bone cement that is compatible with human tissue, or occasionally by encouraging new bone to grow into the artificial joint to secure it in position.

A NEW HIP JOINT

You may think it would be a good idea to trade in your old hip for a new one much as you might a troublesome old car, but your doctor still regards replacement as radical, last stop treatment, only to be considered if all other avenues have been explored. She will want to be absolutely certain that things are not getting any better with available drug treatments before referring you to a surgeon. The orthopaedic surgeon will evaluate how long a replacement joint will have to last in your body and determine the degree of stress to which it will be subjected given your age and normal level of physical activity.

Once your doctor and surgeon have accepted you for an operation, you have to join a long waiting list until a bed is available. Hip replacement operations, however much they revolutionise the life of the arthritis sufferer, do not count as front-line life-saving treatment. Waiting lists for different operations vary at different times and in different parts of the country, but the minimum time you are likely to wait is between three or four months and the longest could be several years.

Once you are actually admitted to hospital there will be a range of tests to gauge your general state of health and suitability for the operation. After the operation the amount of time you will be expected to stay in bed will vary between a few days and a couple of weeks, depending on your personal state of health and the programme favoured by your surgeon. When you do get up on your feet you will need the help of nurses and the physiotherapists to teach you to walk again.

To begin with you will probably be encouraged to put minimal strain on your new hip – no toe-touching or squatting, or sitting in deep, low armchairs. You will be taught how to retrain the muscles that support your new joint with a programme of exercises supervised by the physiotherapist on special equipment available in the ortho-paedic clinic, and later, on your own at home.

You will probably start walking supported by a Zimmer frame or crutches. After a little practice you should progress to a pair of walking sticks and finally, as things become more comfortable and the tissues round your restructured joint repair, you will progress to walking carefully on your own. Most hip replacement patients are back in their own homes within two or three weeks of the operation, depending on the amount of help and support that is available to you there. To begin with you may still need the help of the aids you have had fitted at home to cope with your arthritic hip – raised toilet seat, stair-chair, swivel car seat – but it should be your goal to progress rapidly to a state of independence approaching what you enjoyed before arthritis became a problem.

You will be expected to attend hospital out-patients for routine check-ups and for the physiotherapist to make sure you are using your remodelled hip correctly, but otherwise you will hopefully be away from hospitals for the next 10 or 15 years! Ninety per cent of hip replacement joints are still comfortably in place after this time. X-rays show that hardly any change takes place in the interval. In the unlikely event that you subject it to excessive wear and tear – your steeplechasing days are hopefully over – the whole or part of the joint can easily be replaced.

There can be complications with an intricate piece of metal-work inside your body. There is always a slight statistical risk to life with a general anaesthetic and a lengthy operation in which you may lose quite a lot of blood. The overall risks associated with a hip-replacement operation are about the same as for any major surgical operation. However, a foreign body has been introduced into your own. In a very small number (1%-2%) of cases infection occurs round the artificial joint, often due to some germ that was dormant in your body at the time of the operation. Antibiotics are usually enough to clear things up. There is a small risk of a pulmonary embolism (when a blood clot breaks away from a vein and blocks the entrance to the lungs). This is a hazard common to most operations which surgeons are used to coping with. In earlier hip-replacement operations there was a risk of some loosening of the artificial joint after a time. This is now quite rare and only takes place after many years' good wear.

That said, an artificial joint is never going to be the same as your own hip joint before arthritis set in. However, you yourself are older and are unlikely to notice these deficiencies compared with living with your own hip joint crippled with arthritis. You may never be able to lift your leg as high as you once did, but there is no harm in bending the hip as far as you can, comfortably. Increase your exercise pro-gramme gradually under the guidance of the physiotherapist attached to the hospital or your doctor's clinic. Try and maintain a pattern of normal, but unstrenuous activity: swimming is ideal because it pro-vides exercise for muscles without putting load on the joints; plenty of walking (perhaps not fell-climbing), cycling, dancing and light gardening are all OK. But you should guard against getting your hip into awkward positions. On average you should have about 75% of your previous range of movement in the joint, and there is a 95% chance you will feel absolutely no more pain.

KNEE REPLACEMENT

Many of the things covered in the account of a hip replacement operation also apply to knee replacement. The operation has been around for slightly less time, but the success rate is even higher: 97% of total knee replacements are still working happily after 10 years.

The knee, like the hip, is a very complicated and flexible joint with a wide range of movement; not simply back and forth, like a hinge, as at first might appear, but also quite a degree of twisting takes place in the knee. The three bones that meet at the knee are held together by four ligaments, two in the centre, and one at each side, and by a great deal of 'packing material' to cushion movement that is mostly cartilage – the vulnerable material that so often gets damaged in sporting injuries. When the knee is attacked by osteoarthritis minor surgical treatments like debridement may be tried first, especially if you are still relatively young. If both knees are affected, or if a hip joint (or both) is also affected, there will be the question of in what order your joints should be operated upon. Your age and general fitness, as well as the degree of physical discomfort and restriction of movement you are experiencing in each joint, will be factors influencing these important decisions.

Artificial knee joints have gone through a number of developments in recent years. Initially they were like a simple hinge held together with a pin. This prosthesis had the advantage that it didn't need ligaments to hold it in place, but the movement available was crude compared with a real knee. In practice it worked well only for a short time. A new kind of joint has now been devised that provides new ends to the bones that touch inside the knee but which is held together by your own ligaments. However, the ligaments of someone who has suffered from osteoarthritis are sometimes not up to the job of supporting a new joint and some other solution has to be found. These problems mean that once you have been selected as a candidate for knee replacement the next decision is: what kind of prosthesis?

The preparation for a knee replacement operation may involve a course of special physiotherapy. You may also be advised to lose weight before the operation. This is partly because less body weight means less strain on your new joint, but also because it reduces the risks of the operation itself.

A knee replacement operation is, from the patient's point of view, much the same as a hip replacement, unless you have a spinal anaesthetic rather than a general one. If you do have this kind of anaesthetic – and it avoids the risks associated with total anaesthesia – you will receive an injection that makes your body numb from the hips down. You will be conscious, but comfortably sedated so that you won't become bored or anxious during the two or three hours the surgeons are at work. If you are conscious you will be more aware of what goes on in an operating theatre, unlike the patient under general anaesthetic, and may notice that there is sometimes the need to give a blood transfusion during a lengthy operation like joint replacement. When you return to the ward you may be fitted up with a drip tube into a vein in your arm to help replace the fluid you have lost. Your leg will be in a well-padded bandage or possibly some kind of plaster cast or splint and there may be a thin plastic tube coming out of the joint to allow blood or fluid to drain while the tissues round the new joint begin to repair.

You must be prepared to experience some pain after the operation but you will be given painkillers to cope with this. If you have had a spinal anaesthetic it will take a little time for the movement and feeling to come back to your legs. Recovery time depends to some extent on the kind of knee joint that has been fitted. Sometimes the surgeon will want you to start moving your knee quite soon; in other cases you may be asked to restrain movement for a week or two. When the time comes to start moving, the dressing on your knee will be reduced or removed completely and a physiotherapist will help you start the correct exercise programme. If you are lucky the orthopaedic department will have the use of a hydrotherapy pool where you can do exercises with your body weight supported by water. They may also have a 'passive motion' exerciser, which your leg is strapped to, so that an electric motor can gently bend and straighten the knee without the need for you to use your own muscles and tendons. Ultimately, it will be over to you and your own muscles and the business of learning to walk again.

Rehabilitation after a knee replacement can take longer than with a new hip. There are many variable factors: the kind of joint that has been fitted; the cement used to hold it in place; the hospital department's way of working, and of course your own physical fitness and mental attitude. All these will affect your progress. Be prepared to spend two or three weeks in hospital; quite apart from the nursing care, you have the best physiotherapy facilities at your disposal there.

The physiotherapist will start you walking supported by a Zimmer frame or crutches, or possibly in the hydrotherapy pool with your weight supported by the water. When the time comes to support your own weight your muscles will have begun to build up strength. You may find stairs difficult, and bending or crouching will not be easy for some time. You will obviously never be quite as agile as you were before the arthritis started to affect your joints but most people are extremely satisfied with their operation. It gives relief from pain, excellent freedom of movement and allows you to resume most normal physical activities with ease.

The operation carries with it a slight risk of a clot forming in one of the blood vessels of the leg and you may be prescribed pills for a time to discourage the blood from clotting. There are usually few problems with the joint itself, though the nature of the role demanded of the knee makes a replacement slightly more vulnerable to complications than a hip joint, particularly to start with.

OTHER ARTIFICIAL JOINTS

Artificial joints are being fitted now for the shoulders and elbows, the hand, spine and foot. There is not yet the number of cases there is with hip and knee replacements in order to give you a fair idea of their overall success, but this department of surgery is advancing by leaps and bounds. In the hand, the surgery is particularly delicate and specialised; operations to replace some of the small joints that can be affected by arthritis can now be performed. The spine is also a specialist area. The spinal cord made up of nerve fibres (the life-line for movement and feeling in the body) runs down the middle of the vertebrae, so operations on these bones are usually carried out by neurosurgeons as well as orthopaedic specialists. The removal of a 'slipped disc' – the cushioning cartilage between vertebrae – is the best-known kind of spine surgery. Synthetic discs can also be inserted, and the fusing of two neighbouring vertebrae has been covered under the heading **Bone fusion (arthrodesis)** above.

One of the most common of all orthopaedic operations for arthritis is the removal of bony protrusions at the base of the big toe – a bunion. Other toes become deformed by the arthritis that follows the wear and tear of carrying your body around for years and years, as well as the pressure from tight or unsuitable shoes. The toe joints can also become seriously damaged by rheumatoid arthritis and require removal and replacement. This operation is popular and successful and offers good pain relief.

THE FUTURE

It is our primary objective in this book to give you a positive approach to managing arthritis. But it is impossible to end a chapter on what the doctors can do for you without being aware that the treatments we have described are complicated, bedevilled with side-effects and, with the possible exception of gout, incomplete. We have concerned ourselves with what is available now, because that is what you have to choose from, but there is much that the doctors may be able to offer you in the near future.

Several lines of medical research hold out great hope for improved treatments, even a possible cure, for rheumatoid arthritis within a matter of years. They are the result of bio-engineering techniques you may have read about in the newspapers. Basically, it means that scientists can now take living cell material responsible for very precise tasks in the human body, grow it and alter it in the laboratory, possibly produce quite new varieties, then put it back into the body to change the process of disease.

Mono-clonal antibodies (mAbs). Don't worry too much about the precise meaning of the name of this new bio-engineered disease-fighting cell. The important part of its name is the 'mono' meaning one, or single. MAbs are designed in the laboratory so that they attach themselves to one specific site in the body. It's like turning off a single tap, rather than the water supply at the mains. In the case of rheumatoid arthritis, they are targeted to interrupt at a precise point in the complex chain reaction which is responsible for the inflammation of the joint membrane. They offer an alternative to having to turn off the entire auto-immune protection system with a general immunosuppressant, with the risk of exposing the body to other forms of infection. MAbs are being produced that will protect the part of the immune system that gets attacked, or knock out the part that does the attacking. There are some half a dozen mAbs in development operating in many different ways to halt the process underlying the disease.

Some mAbs are already being tested for safety in people suffering from rheumatoid arthritis. As with all new drugs, they have been tried first on patients with long-standing disease who have failed to respond to existing treatments. The signs are that they are safe, with only brief side-effects and will turn out to be particularly effective for people at the early stages of the disease.

An American rheumatologist, quoted in the specialist publication *Pharmaceutical Visions* in November 1992, hazarded a guess that the first mAbs for rheumatoid arthritis might be on the market in three to five years. The same specialist said hopefully that bio-engineering will eventually identify the gene that someone carries that makes them susceptible to the disease. "It's a lock and key situation", he explained; "We've been looking all along for the key – that is, what might trigger the disease." But identifying a key tells you a lot about the shape of the lock. And the 'lock' in rheumatoid arthritis is ultimately the thing that lets the disease in when the key is inserted.

8 Devices And Gadgets

An enormous array of aids exists to make the arthritis sufferer's life easier in every respect. Clever devices can help you to bath, to dress, to drive your car, to make life at work more comfortable, to shop, to cook, to do the housework, and even to do some relaxing gardening. No arthritis sufferer should shrink from taking advantage of anything that helps.

It's worth noting, however, that all the devices and gadgets described in this chapter are intended to assist you with those tasks that you really cannot perform alone. They are not meant to relieve you of useful bending and stretching movements, provided that you can still perform those. Try, then, to manage without for as long as you can, until you are certain that you need them, or your doctor or physiotherapist assures you that you can no longer derive any benefit from managing without help.

Taking the pain and strain out of everyday tasks as simple as opening a can or turning on a tap need not be expensive. Many of these gadgets and aids are quite inexpensive and can revolutionise your life, erasing frustration and pain.

HANDY ABOUT THE HOUSE

There is an enormous range of equipment from which you can pick and choose items that are useful to have around your home. These include a long pole with pincers at the end so that you can pick up things without having to bend or stoop (Reacher from *Damart*), a walking stick, an infra-red massager (*Damart*) or Back Doctor (*The Back Shop*), a foot massager (rows of wooden balls to roll your feet over), a leg relaxer or footstool, a neck cushion for support while relaxing or watching TV, and a pedal exerciser (*Damart*). These are just some examples of the things you can buy (by mail order if necessary) from one of four major suppliers (all details at the end of this book). *The Disabled Living Foundation* and *The Arthritis and Rheumatism Council* are also tremendously knowledgeable about gadgets.

The Back Shop is a specialist shop for back sufferers and carries a large number of useful items for arthritis sufferers, including adjustable chairs, tilting and adjustable tables, back and foot massagers and exercisers. Some of their special chairs are quite revolutionary in design and well worth trying.

John Bell & Croyden is a well-stocked chemist and medical aids store for the public and the medical profession. Here you will find a wide range of bathroom equipment for the disabled, including special loos, loo seats and portable male urinals (to save male sufferers getting up in the night). They also stock special chairs and tilting tables, wheelchairs, shopping trolleys and even a lambswool bed pad to protect your feet (specially good for gout sufferers) and your elbow joints while asleep.

Damart are probably best known for their warm underwear (which, as many of us know, Princess Diana has said she would not be without). They also stock, however, a good range of gadgets for the arthritis sufferer for use about the house, in the kitchen, in the car and in the garden.

Keep Able specialise, as their name implies, in a range of goods to help the disabled, including bathroom equipment, devices for the bedroom and about the house (including a range of Handreachers), wheelchairs, a four-wheeled shopping scooter, and tables of all sizes in adjustable heights and on castors.

Between them, these four stockists should be able to supply you with most of the things described in this chapter.

KEEP WARM

Before we look at equipment to help you in your specific everyday activities, it's worth remembering that you should keep warm at all times. Five minutes a day limbering up exercises should get your circulation moving, and you should then be able to keep warm with cosy underwear from *Damart*. They have lacy vests and long pants (they are much more attractive than they used to be) and they also stock warm socks and fleecy boots, as well as fleecy slippers. If you let yourself become chilly, there will be even less movement in your joints.

GETTING UP IN THE MORNING

We have already described in Chapter 3 the need for a good comfortable bed, in order to eliminate unnecessary aches and pains. You may also find a posture pillow (*Damart*) useful. Keeping warm is, again, an important consideration, so think about a heated under-blanket and/or a heated overblanket.

If you feel stiff in the morning and find it difficult to get up, lie on your side, swing your legs over the edge of the bed, use your arm to push your torso upwards and, as you do so, touch the floor with your feet. Still keeping your back straight, ease yourself up, at first taking your weight on your arm, then using it to push your body into an upright position.

Incidentally, if it takes you a while to get up, you will find it useful to have a commode (*Keep Able*) near your bed, and perhaps a push-button (not dial) telephone (from your local Phone Shop, listed in your telephone directory).

Making the bed is easier if you use a fitted bottom sheet and a duvet to save you the effort of tucking in voluminous sheets and heavy blankets. A bed cradle takes the weight off painful feet and knees and is specially useful for gout sufferers.

TAKING A BATH

First of all, you may wish to consider switching to a shower as this could make life much easier. For extra safety, invest in a special chair to sit upon in the shower. Whether you bath or shower, some of these will be useful:

- Grip- or grab-rail fixed to the side of the bath.
- Non-slip mat for either bath or shower.
- Bath seat.
- Lever bath taps (much easier to operate than the conventional domestic ones).
- Long-handled back brush, long loofah and long-handled sponge.
- Nail brush with suction pads (it adheres to the bath surface and you brush your nails against it rather than having to curl your fingers around it).
- Bath head rest.
- Soap on a rope.
- A bath mitten rather than a flannel (much easier for stiff fingers).
- Heated towel rail for a nice warm towel.

THE LOO

Those shops carrying bathroom equipment for the disabled stock special seats to fit over your existing loo seat in order to raise it. This is particularly helpful for those with stiff hips and knees. Most medical aids stockists can sell you a long-handled wiper with the lavatory paper wrapped around the rubber end. A grip-rail by the side of the loo is also useful.

GETTING DRESSED

Chapter 3 offered some tips to avoid causing yourself unnecessary effort and pain. The cardinal rule is to avoid bending and twisting as much as possible: much better to dress as effortlessly as possible and then carry out your limbering up routine (*see Chapter 4*).

So, go for cardigans rather than sweaters, shirts or blouses in easy-care fabric rather than T-shirts, skirts with elasticated waists rather than fiddly zips. Side or back zip skirts can be done up at the front and then slid round your waist. If you have a favourite dress that zips up the back, see if your local dry cleaners can convert it to a side zip, which will be just a little easier. A tricky zip can still be done up with the aid of a piece of string looped through the catch and pulled up. Tights are warmer and easier to put on than stockings: you don't have to twist to do up the back suspenders. When you buy shoes, avoid laces and go for a comfortable slip-on that gives you enough support. A long-handled shoehorn will prove invaluable: once you have one, you may wonder how you ever did without it. Also useful is a device for pulling up socks and stockings.

Whenever you buy new clothes or shoes, or jewellery for that matter, if the assistant springs to your aid to help you with a fastening, politely decline her help and explain that you need to be able to do it yourself. Don't buy if you cannot manage it.

Check out your cupboard and wardrobe arrangements: shoes littering the bottom of your wardrobe may prove a source of frustration. It would be better to have them hanging in polythene holders suspended on the inside of the doors at, or just above, your waist height.

COPING WITH THE CHILDREN

If you are unfortunate enough to be suffering with arthritis while also having very young children, it would be worth avoiding lace-up shoes for them, too, as you would otherwise have to tie the laces for them. Choose for them the simplest possible clothes with the minimum of buttons, zips and bows so that they soon learn to dress themselves. Tracksuits with elasticated waists would be ideal. Children are by nature independent and explorative, and therefore they usually much prefer to do things for themselves in any case.

If you have a young baby, you will need a cot with a let-down side so that you don't have to lean over and pick her up. (This would place the maximum strain on your joints and your back.) Consider investing in a baby bath on a frame so that you can bath her without stooping. Feed her in a high chair, with you seated upon a chair next to her, in order to avoid, again, stooping.

DRIVING WITH ARTHRITIS

If you are suffering from acute arthritis, you won't feel like driving, and in any case it's better not to. However, provided you are not in too much pain, you should be all right, as long as you ensure you are seated as comfortably as possible.

Remember, if you are driving and have recently become an arthritis sufferer, the law requires that if the illness both affects your driving and has lasted more than three months you must inform the *Drivers Medical Branch, DVLC, Swansea*. It's possible you may be asked to take a further test. If you are applying for a provisional licence, you have to declare you are an arthritis sufferer, but don't let that put you off because disabled drivers, although they have to achieve the same standard as other motorists, are often allowed extra time.

If you have to wear splints or a collar, ask your doctor if you should wear them when you are driving. If you experience dizzy spells when you turn your neck (either because of the collar or because of the drugs you are taking), you shouldn't be driving. Ask your doctor if any of the pills you take are likely to affect your driving. If this is the case, either avoid taking them before you set off, or don't drive. If possible, take any pills that may ease the pain before you drive, provided that they do not induce drowsiness. Here again, you must get advice from your doctor.

For severe arthritis sufferers, it's a good plan to visit a mobility assessment unit. The *Mobility Information Service* (address at the end of the book) will advise you on your nearest one and also provide other valuable information on request. You may think it worth contacting the Department of Transport, because they have test roads in Berkshire with different types of adapted cars for you to try.

You may be able to get an orange parking badge which means you'll be able to park closer to shops. Your local Social Services Department will be able to advise you on this.

If you are about to buy a new or second-hand car, you should consider one with power steering and an automatic gear box. Light steering is a great bonus if you have arthritis, and automatic gears take a lot of the effort out of driving. Do ensure that your car's shock absorbers are in good condition so that you don't suffer painful jolts.

The standard fitted seat belts may present a problem because, usually, you have to twist to fasten them. The solution is an easy-reach belt, an extension to the standard one, which eliminates the need to twist round. You can have custom-made alterations to your car, such as swivelling seats, wheelchair hoists or steering wheel knobs, and these can be fitted by specialist garages.

The first step is actually getting into the car, and if you do this in the wrong way it can be painful. Do it the Royal way: you're in excellent company here because this is the way the Queen gets into a car. Open the door, sit sideways on the seat so that your left side faces the steering wheel, and then swing your legs around into the car.

Make a mental note always to use this method, whether you're the driver or a passenger, as it ensures that your spine and the joints of your body are not forced to make an uncomfortable twist.

If you're a passenger and suffering from acute arthritis which restricts your leg movements, you should ask the driver to help you lift your legs into the car.

When you're in the car, do check the position of the seat and the headrest (an essential item). Use the following points as a guideline to finding the correct position:

- You shouldn't have to stretch unduly to reach the pedal controls.
- Make sure you aren't cramped as this affects blood circulation, particularly to your joints, and this can result in pain and stiffness.

- Your back should feel well supported. Tuck your bottom well into the back of the seat. Your back should be upright and at right angles to your thighs.
- The seat shouldn't be angled backwards, as this encourages you to slouch over the wheel for support.
- Check the headrest to make sure your neck and upper spine are firmly supported. A good headrest is important because it stops your head being thrown back if you have to brake suddenly and therefore helps to prevent whiplash.
- If your seat isn't comfortable, you may have to buy a portable car seat, or a heated one.
- Before the start of any journey, check the rear view and wing mirrors are properly adjusted to suit your height without having to stretch, twist or dip your head.

There are all sorts of extras you can buy that will make driving easier:

- A small blind-spot mirror that clips onto the driver's wing mirror is available from *Damart* and most garages. It's wide angled, fully adjustable, and will avoid your having to make awkward movements.
- *Damart* also offers a wooden seat massager. The wooden beads mould to the shape of your back and give a gentle massage on your journey.
- A padded steering wheel cover will make gripping the wheel easier and less painful for people with arthritic hands.
- A scraper mitt will keep your hand warm while you clear the windscreen of snow and ice in bad weather; and a heated scraper which simply plugs into your car's cigarette lighter socket, makes it easy to remove snow and ice and helps to make sure your hands stay warm.
- An anti-mist mitt, which is specially impregnated, stops car windows steaming up (*Damart*).

- A clip board with a suction pad for the dashboard (*Damart*) means that you can have your shopping list and map or whatever to hand.

Remember never to drive when you're tired, and try to make it a rule not to drive for longer than an hour at a time. Get out and stretch your legs to avoid stiffness and keep the joints supple.

When you come to get out of the car, release your seat belt, open the door, swing your legs to the right so that you are sitting sideways on the seat with your feet poised over the road, and then move out and straighten up.

AT WORK

If your arthritis is fairly mild and manageable, you may still be working. In this case, the important points to remember are:

- Keep yourself warm enough, even if it means taking an extra cardigan in to keep at your place of work.
- Move around every half an hour or so, so that your joints don't seize up and your circulation keeps moving. Beware sitting in front of a computer terminal for hours on end! If, however, your job is very sedentary, then rotate your feet and hands in the air now and again to keep them as supple as possible.
- Your desk height in relation to the height of your chair is very important. You should not have to reach up to a computer terminal or typewriter. Your arms at rest should form a right angle to your body. When you are seated, your legs should not dangle just above the floor: if the chair is too high for you but at the correct height to your desk, ask for a footstool (or bring in your own) or improvise with a box beneath the desk. If your chair is too high for the length of your legs, the chair edge will press on the back of your thighs and thus impede your circulation, and may cause swollen puffy ankles.
- Avoid carrying heavy loads. Try and split them into several smaller loads if you can, and make more trips. If this is impossible, don't

hesitate to ask for help – people usually like to be of assistance to others.

- Be sure to get a good walk at break times and at lunchtime. Moderate exercise in fresh air will be beneficial to you.

THE SHOPPING

If you are severely disabled, you will clearly need a wheelchair and some assistance. A four-wheeled shopping scooter is available from *Keep Able*. If your arthritis is fairly mild, you will be able to shop for yourself, bearing in mind these points: don't overdo it as fatigue will increase aches and pains, and don't attempt to carry too much.

The best way to avoid having to carry heavy loads of shopping is to observe as many as possible of the following suggestions:

- Go on two or three small shopping trips per week instead of one large one.
- Wear insoles in your shoes to reduce jolting to the spine and joints, which will increase when you carry heavy shopping.
- Use a shopping trolley on wheels instead of a basket or bags.
- If you cannot use a trolley, use several bags evenly distributed, rather than carrying one heavy one in one hand which throws your spine and hips out of alignment.
- If you shop at a supermarket, use the trolleys provided. If you happen to use a wire basket, do not attempt to swing it up onto the surface by the cash register. Unload it first, item by item, or ask someone else to lift it for you.
- If you find that you have such a heavy load that you are unsure whether you can carry it safely, then leave half of it with an assistant, explaining that you will return later to collect it.
- With heavier items, always ask the shop if they will deliver. If they will not, and the item is definitely too heavy for you, ask a friend or neighbour to pick it up with their car.

IN THE KITCHEN

This is the room in which we perform more twisting, bending and intricate movements than in any other. Even turning on a tap or unplugging a kettle can pose a serious problem to the arthritis sufferer.

First and foremost, make sure that everything is at the most convenient height for you. Move the things that you use the most from very low shelves or cupboards: consider, too, whether you can achieve more storage space at waist height. A small table-top refrigerator will be more use to you than a full size floor-standing model.

- Plug sockets can be moved from skirting level to your waist height, or you could use extension leads.

- Long-handled tools, such as a long-handled dustpan and brush, a long-handled broom and a long-handled duster, will prove invaluable.

- Place insoles in your shoes, particularly if your kitchen floor is uncarpeted, to reduce jarring to your joints and spine.

- Avoid picking up heavy loads: split them up and carry several lighter loads instead. Alternatively, invest in a small waist-height trolley.

- If you need to reach high cupboards, use a small 3-rung stepladder in preference to a stool which tends to be less stable.

- Have your vegetable rack fixed to the wall at waist height rather than on the floor.

- You will find it easier to manage lever taps in preference to the conventional screw taps.

- Use a wall-mounted can opener to save you using a conventional tin opener (try it before you buy).

- Fit a tea dispenser to the wall so that you don't have to grapple with a tin and a spoon every time you fancy a cup of tea. Ideally, use teabags.

- In order not to risk picking up a heavy saucepan of boiling water each time your vegetables are ready, either remove the vegetables with a slotted spoon or place them in a wire basket (like a chip basket) before putting them in water to boil.

- Keep any heavy equipment, such as a food mixer, on one of your surfaces or easy-to-reach shelves, rather than at the bottom of a cupboard where it will prove awkward and heavy to retrieve.
- Throw out a swing bin as, when full, it will be heavy and cumbersome to take out to empty. Use instead a pedal bin so that you are emptying light loads more frequently.
- If you can afford a dishwasher, washing up and energetic scouring will become a thing of the past. Dishwashers these days can cope with virtually everything other than bone-handled cutlery, wooden implements and plates incorporating gold in the pattern (the heat and dishwasher liquid combine to wear away the gold).

Whatever you do, don't overdo it: if you feel tired, stop and have a rest.

CLEANING YOUR HOME

Once again, long-handled tools come into their own:

- A long-handled duster is indispensable. So, too, is a long-handled cobweb brush.
- If you find that a vacuum cleaner is becoming too heavy and awkward to manage, try instead a light carpet sweeper (these are often found cheaply through the Articles for Sale column in your local newspaper).
- Spray polishes will produce as good a result as beeswax and old-fashioned elbow grease.
- Mirrors and windows can all be cleaned with a long-handled sponge.

WASHING AND IRONING

- Empty the washing machine little by little in small light loads so that you are not faced with carrying a heavy load.

- Hang the clothes over drying racks indoors if you find it too tricky to manage a washing line.
- Some people find it easier to sit at an ironing board, while others find it preferable to stand. Whichever suits you, make sure that the board is at the correct height for your hands and arms. You should be able to iron without bending your arm too much. If you have the space, leave the board up permanently so that you don't have to bother setting it up and collapsing it every time you wish to iron.

IN THE GARDEN

A day spent in the garden is a notorious cause of all sorts of aches and pains. Personally, my feelings about gardening are best expressed by someone called Charles Barr. He said, in 1948, of this greatly loved activity: "The best way to enjoy the garden is to put on a wide straw hat, hold a little trowel in one hand and a cool drink in the other, and tell the man where to dig!".

Actually, gardening is an excellent chance to enjoy moderate exercise in the fresh air, as it will invigorate you and tone up tired muscles.

You need to approach it, however, with a lot of thought and care. Whether your whole body is affected by arthritis, or just one joint, you may find bending, or generally just getting around, difficult.

The important things are:

- Vary your activities, and aim to move from one job to another every five to ten minutes, so that you do not have to maintain an unaccustomed or uncomfortable posture for any length of time.
- Think about how you move: for example, when digging you should be as close to the fork or spade as possible. And weed from a sitting or kneeling position, as bending double can be excruciating for the joints.
- Select long-handled, lightweight tools and implements.

- A gardener, whose stiff knee is only a slight problem when he/she is digging, can change their method in order to put less strain on the knee, but someone who has more severe arthritis, perhaps in several joints, may have to accept working from a stool or a wheelchair.
- Don't forget the golden rule is to *keep warm*! It's best in winter to wear one hundred per cent wool underclothing and thick woollen socks, fleecy gardening gloves and a woollen hat, rather than relying on a bulky jacket. Do wear good shoes with non-skid soles to avoid the risk of a fall.
- Give some thought to the layout of the garden: paved paths alongside beds and borders make good sense, and you might even consider replacing your lawn with paving stones to cut out the need for mowing.

USEFUL TIPS

- Garden centres will be able to give you lots of good, helpful advice on layout, and help you choose easy-care perennial shrubs.
- You can buy fruit trees that have been grafted onto dwarf root-stocks, which restricts their growth and means the fruit is easily reachable.
- Choose a half-moon border spade rather than a full size spade. It's lighter and a lot easier to handle.
- A utility cart on castors is available from *Damart*, which is perfect for any job that involves kneeling. It has a seat with a tray which holds all the tools you need.
- *Damart* also sell lightweight kneepads which give good padded protection when you are on your knees.
- Invest in long-handled shears, electric long-handled border trimmers, long-handled pruners, long-handled apple pickers and long-handled weed extractors. The long-handled weed extractor is particularly worthwhile since weeding in the summer is a weekly

chore. With this handy tool, you push a strong, sharp harpoon with a long handle into the ground, give half a turn and lift out the weed complete with its roots.

- It's also possible to buy a set of tools which are designed to be attached to a long, snap-lock handle (*Damart*). This saves space and ensures minimum wear and tear to your joints. A set might include, for example, a soil miller, a seed sower, a rake, a push-pull weeder and a cultivator.

- When it comes to cutting the grass, opt for a lightweight mower – there are several on the market. Use an attachment to pick up the mown grass so that you don't have to rake it up later. Better still, if you mow frequently, don't collect the grass at all. Just let it go back into the soil; it's all added nutrients.

- You would be wise to invest in a hose (if you don't have one already) so that you can avoid lugging a heavy watering can around.

- Most gardeners have a wheelbarrow. Anyone with arthritis should beware of using the ordinary low-handled type. Instead, get a lightweight plastic barrow with a removable plastic box on a tubular steel frame. You can purchase one that has two wheels and a single long handle which is very easy to manage and avoids the need to bend down or twist when you empty it.

- Plant containers that are high enough off the ground enable you to work conveniently.

- Any heavy plant tubs should be mounted on castors so that you can move them without difficulty.

- Lastly, take care not to overdo it, to avoid a painful flare-up of your condition.

RELAXING

Enough of gardening and housework! What you need in your sitting room is a comfortable, supporting armchair (not too low in order to minimise the strain on your joints when you wish to get up), a footstool, a massage pillow, a hand trainer, a back massager and a pedal exerciser. (All are available from *Damart* or *The Back Shop*.)

Deep, sloppy armchairs and poor posture will put an enormous strain on tired joints, so take care to avoid these. Try and resist the temptation to sit for too long at a time, as this is likely to cause your circulation to slow and your joints and spine to seize up. Get up and move about every now and then.

AND, EVENTUALLY, TO BED . . .

One of the most fulfilling activities in our lives, and perhaps the most likely to induce a deep sense of well-being, is making love with one's partner. As one grows older, lovemaking may become less frequent, but no less satisfying for that. Many people in their seventies and eighties still enjoy an active sex life. Arthritis sufferers may experience some discomfort and, as a consequence, some loss of desire. However, that is no reason to give up completely one of life's most satisfying activities. It's important, too, to show your partner your affection and love and not to risk neglecting him/her as a result of your own health problems. The easiest position for both of you is to lie on your sides, both facing the same way, so that you assume the shape of two spoons next to each other.

If you, as the woman, suffer painful hips and knees, you will not easily be able to sit astride your partner, but you will probably be able to manage the conventional 'missionary' position unless you are severely disabled. If this is the case, show your love through affection, hugs, kisses and manual methods of satisfying your partner. He can do the same for you, too.

Conclusion

A bove all, the message of hope to all arthritis sufferers is in the ways you can help yourself through knowledge and the practical advice we have given. This book contains detailed information on the different types of arthritis and ways of fighting it, ranging from drugs to diet and exercise.

These days, there is a change of attitude in general. Doctors and the different types of therapists involved now applaud patient involvement. The words of rheumatologist, Ian Haslock, in a recent edition of *Doctor* journal, are worth repeating:

"Patients have higher expectations nowadays. In the past, they were willing to be fobbed off with the advice 'there's nothing can be done for arthritis', and would accept progressive disability as an inevitable consequence of their disease. They are now more knowledgeable and generally less tolerant of symptoms."

Knowing about arthritis and the different treatment options that are available is a large part of the battle. Of course, it's difficult to plan a strategy unless you know what lies ahead. Many of you afflicted by the disease will have heard or read somewhere that it is incurable. That in itself is a body blow to the greatest optimist, and really doesn't bear out the truth. As we have said, the object of researchers is to understand the way that arthritis affects our joints so that they can develop means of reversing the damage or preventing further damage occurring.

Treating the symptoms, however, can limit damage to affected joints so that arthritis may go into remission: there may then be a prolonged, maybe an indefinite, period without pain and with full mobility. This can be achieved through sensible medical advice and the use of drugs, but also, very importantly, through an awareness of the ways in which you can help yourself.

Don't just glance through these chapters, read and then re-read them. Quite naturally, most people tend to panic when they are told that they have an illness such as this. But once you absorb the facts and discover what can be done, it should help you take a calmer approach. You can then think constructively about what can be done by those responsible for your care, and about the things you can do to help yourself.

Firstly, you're not alone. It's common for all of us to suffer from aches, pains and stiffness from childhood onwards, and most of us will develop some form of arthritis at some time in our lives. There are countless numbers of people who are putting up with the misery of unnecessary pain who probably are totally unaware that they are arthritis sufferers. Remember, this is a disease that can strike anyone, from healthy teenagers and sportsmen to pensioners.

Fortunately, doctors' attitudes are changing towards their patients, and there is a greater public awareness of our right to prompt and effective treatment since the advent of the Citizen's Charter. So, you will probably find that your doctor is far more sympathetic than you'd imagined in listening to your complaints.

If you believe that you have any of the symptoms of arthritis, don't hesitate to go to your doctor for help. Don't, for a moment, take the attitude, "The doctor's so busy, I don't like to bother him or her". You should know from reading the first two chapters whether or not you are a sufferer. For instance, sitting in the cold for any length of time is going to cause aches and pains but that is not arthritis, and playing a sport, such as tennis, may result in tennis elbow and that is not arthritis either, but a specific sports injury. The important point to note is whether or not you are suffering persistent pain in any particular joint in your day-to-day activities.

Once you visit your doctor, you shouldn't be too alarmed if a particular type of arthritis is diagnosed. The most common types are described at the beginning of the book in such a way that we hope it will help everyone's understanding.

Chapter 3, *Relief From Pain*, emphasises, once again, the message that there's hope for us all. Yes, it used to be (and, sadly, sometimes still is) the case that arthritis sufferers were given no help or guidance on how to cope with their day-to-day problems, apart from taking drugs for the relief of pain.

Learning to live with and minimise pain by rest, relaxation techniques and exercise is all-important. We've given you a clear and detailed guide on the different ways of producing good results – but, of course, you have to find your own balance.

It's important with exercise to appreciate that everyone is different – according to their age, weight and level of fitness. So don't push yourself too hard, start gradually and build up. And, if you feel tired, take a rest. Don't overdo it! Concentrate, in your exercise regime, on developing a routine that you feel happy with. It's vital that you establish a rhythmic routine in order to increase the elasticity and strength of all your joints.

There are tremendous gains for arthritis sufferers to be achieved through visualisation and meditation. Many people think that these valuable forms of therapy are far more difficult, inaccessible or esoteric than they actually are. That's probably because they tend to be associated with the mystique of the Tibetan monks and Indian gurus who have practised such techniques for centuries. But don't be put off: these techniques are actually very easy ways of achieving relaxation and some pain relief without drugs, and just require practice.

Much the same applies to yoga from which you can achieve wonderful results in a fairly short space of time. You will be able to find classes or activity groups for these special techniques to fit your needs, and they're easy to find out about through your doctor, local library, town hall, hospital physiotherapy department, or via the contact addresses at the end of this book. There's no need to feel shy about joining one of these classes; remember there will be others there with similar problems, so you will be able to exchange help, support and useful tips.

The simple common sense things are of inestimable help. Into this category come tips and gadgets, some of which are so simple once we know about them. Little things can make a huge difference, such as, for example, using a sponge at bathtime instead of a flannel because it readily absorbs more water; using a long-handled comb; and, wearing flat rather than high-heeled shoes.

Most office managers now are conscious of the importance of providing chairs and stools that provide the correct support; but, if you happen to work in an office where this isn't the case, make them aware of your problem. We've mentioned the importance of having the right bed, but beware of advertisements for orthopaedic beds. If your present one is unsuitable, ask your physiotherapist for advice.

Eating the right foods and finding a suitable diet can play a vital role in helping arthritis. Although we've stressed there is no miracle cure for the disease, different American doctors have claimed astonishing results through changing their eating habits entirely. For instance, Dr Collin Dong, a Californian who was stricken with arthritis when he was thirty-five, says that conventional drugs didn't work for him, but eating only wholefoods saved him from a wheel-chair.

It's certainly true that avoiding junk food and red meat, and eating more vegetables and fruit, is healthier for all of us, so changing your diet in this way may well produce favourable results. Do make a point of keeping a systematic day-to-day list of your dietary changes so that you can see which appear to have positive results.

By far the most valuable change in diet for overweight people with arthritis, is a reduction in intake of food in general. Nothing places more strain on inflamed joints than too much weight. So, if you are carrying more than the ideal weight for your height (*see Chapter 5*), do make it a priority to lose it – slowly but surely.

If you suffer from arthritis, you will have to make a number of changes to your life-style in almost every area. We hope this book has shown you how.

ACKNOWLEDGEMENT

I would like to endorse the excellent work carried out by *The Arthritis and Rheumatism Council*, which relies entirely on voluntary contributions to fund its extensive research projects and provide support and encouragement to arthritis sufferers. I also thank them for their help with this book.

USEFUL ORGANISATIONS

Arthritis Care, 18, Stephenson Way, London NW1 2HD. Telephone: 071-916 1500.

The Arthritis and Rheumatism Council for Research, PO Box 177, Chesterfield, Derbyshire S41 7TQ. Telephone: 0246 558033.

Back Pain Association, Grundy House, 31-33 Park Road, Teddington, Middlesex TW11 0AB. Telephone: 081-977 5474.

Centre for Accessible Environment, 35 Great Smith Street, London SW1P 3BJ. Telephone: 071-222 7980.

Disabled Drivers' Association, Central Office, Ashwellthorpe Hall, Ashwellthorpe, Norwich NR16 1EX. Telephone: 0508 41449.

The Disabled Living Foundation, 380-384 Harrow Road, London W9 2HU. Telephone: 071-289 6111.

The Mobility Information Service, National Mobility Centre, MOTEC, High Ercall, Telford, Shropshire TF6 6RB. Telephone: 0952 770881.

National Ankylosing Spondylitis Society, 5 Grosvenor Crescent, London SW1X 7ER. Telephone: 071-235 9585.

The Royal Association for Disability and Rehabilitation, 25 Mortimer Street, London W1N 8AB. Telephone: 071-637 5400.

CONTACT ADDRESSES FOR CHAPTER 6

Acupuncture
British Acupuncture Association and Register, 34 Alderney Street, London SW1V 4EU. Telephone: 071-834 1012.

Alexander Technique
Society of Teachers of the Alexander Technique, 20 London House, 266 Fulham Road, London SW10 9EL. Telephone: 071-351 0828.

Aromatherapy
The International Federation of Aromatherapists, Royal Masonic Hospital, Ravenscourt Park, London W6 0TN. Telephone: 081-846 8066.

Bach Flower Remedies
Bach Centre, Mount Vernon, Sotwell, Wallingford, Oxfordshire OX10 0PZ. Telephone: 0491 39489.

Chiropractic
British Chiropractic Association, 29 Whitley Street, Reading, Berkshire RG2 0EG. Telephone: 0734 757557.

Medical Herbalists
The National Institute of Medical Herbalists, 9 Palace Gate, Exeter EX1 1JA. Telephone: 0392 426022.

Homoeopathy
The Hahnemann Society, Hahnemann House, 2 Powis Place, Great Ormond Street, London WC1N 3HT. Telephone: 071-837 3297.

Hypnotherapy

British Hypnotherapy Association, 1 Wythburn Place, London W1H 5WL. Telephone: 071-723 4443.

Osteopathy

The General Council and Register of Osteopaths, 56 London Street, Reading, Berkshire RG1 4SQ. Telephone: 0734 576585.

Reflexology

The Association of Reflexologists, 27 Old Gloucester Street, London WC1N 3XX. Telephone: 071-237 6523.

Shiatsu

The Shiatsu Society of Great Britain, 14 Oakdene Road, Redhill, Surrey RH1 6BT. Telephone: 0737 767896.

Yoga

British Wheel of Yoga, 1 Hamilton Place, Boston Road, Sleaford, Lincolnshire NG34 7ES. Telephone: 0529 306851.

The Iyengar Yoga Institute, 223a Randolph Avenue, London W9 1NL. Telephone: 071-624 3080.

SHOPS WITH MAIL ORDER FACILITIES

The Back Shop, 24 New Cavendish Street, London W1M 7LH. Telephone: 071-935 9120.

John Bell & Croyden Chemists, 52-54 Wigmore Street, London W1H 0AU. Telephone: 071-935 5555.

Damart, Bowling Green Mills, Bingley, West Yorkshire BD16 3ZD. Telephone: 0274 568211.

Keep Able, 2 Capital Interchange Way, nr Kew Bridge, Brentford, Middlesex TW8 0EX. Telephone: 081-742 2181. (Catalogue from Fleming Close, Park Farm, Wellingborough, Northamptonshire NN8 6UF. Telephone: 0933 679426.)

Personal Arthritis Record

Personal Arthritis Record